WHY "FLIRTING" LEADS TO SUCCESS

❏

Say the word "flirting" and everybody assumes you're talking about romance. But, can flirting be used to achieve career goals? Can it be a legitimate business asset?

"Yes, it can," says award-winning motivational speaker Jill Spiegel. "We all know that the key to achieving goals in a career and elsewhere is the ability to make sincere connections with people." Now this dynamic entrepreneur teaches you how to develop and hone your natural abilities for building personality bridges, establishing rapport, and achieving your goals by FLIRTING FOR SUCCESS. Turn the page for seminar-proven techniques that will enable you to:

- Inspire confidence in yourself and others
- Use humor to your advantage
- Build lasting and trusting relationships
- Negotiate effectively
- Captivate interest
- Achieve professional and personal goals.

❏

"A must for anyone who wants to effectively build rapport!"

**—Troy Prickett,
marketing manager, Sony Music**

"Spiegel achieves her business goals by helping others achieve theirs first."

—*Career Woman* magazine

❏

FLIRTING
FOR
SUCCESS
THE ART OF BUILDING RAPPORT

JILL SPIEGEL

WARNER BOOKS

A Time Warner Company

Warner Books Edition
Copyright © 1994 by Jill Spiegel
All rights reserved.

This Warner Books edition is published by arrangement with the author.

Warner Books, Inc., 1271 Avenue of the Americas, New York, NY 10020

Ⓦ A Time Warner Company

Printed in the United States of America
First Warner Books Printing: May 1995
10 9 8 7 6 5 4 3 2 1

Library of Congress Cataloging-in-Publication Data

Spiegel, Jill.
    Flirting for success : the art of building rapport / Jill Spiegel.
        p. cm.
    Originally publihed: St. Paul, Minn. : Macalester Park Pub.,
1994
    ISBN 0-446-67180-0
    1. Success in business. 2. Interpersonal communication.
3. Interpersonal relations. 4. Self-presentation. 5. Public relations.
I. Title.
HF 5386.S752 1995
650. 1—dc20   94-41479
                                               CIP

Cover design by Wendy Bass Design
Cover photograph by Mark Bloom

DEDICATION

This book is dedicated to my incredible husband, Joe, whose patience, support, understanding, and strength made this project and me possible. I still can't believe how lucky I am.

My sister. Sally, you are, without a doubt, the greatest sister anyone could have. Thanks for always loving, protecting, and "being there" for me.

My parents, Sue and Andy (Ma and Cluff). I wish everybody could experience your amazing sense of humor, your youthful enthusiasm for everything around you, and your refreshing and heartfelt appreciation for people. You've taught me a lot!

To all the people who have nurtured this project: Mike Beard, David Wexler, Jeff Braun, Jane McLain, Denise Gjerde, Rob McQuilkin, Jamie Raab, and everbody at Warner Books. "Thanks" isn't enough. To my close friends and colleagues who have given unyielding support. And thanks to all the role models and people who have shown me that connecting with one another is what life is all about.

TABLE OF CONTENTS

1

FLIRTING IS . . .

Flirting is good people skills
Flirting helps negotiating
Flirting builds self-esteem

Wait a minute. Something doesn't sound right. For years, we have understood flirting to mean a romantic or sexual game between people who are physically attracted to each other. You know, the "slick lines," winks, subtle innuendos, and so on. But, flirting to achieve goals? Flirting in business?

Yes, it's true. We all know that the key to achieving goals in a career and elsewhere is the ability to make sincere connections with people. An ability which happens to come naturally. But, as you look at your past education, you won't recall any textbook, class, or seminar that taught you how to make those connections. And you may wonder, does flirting come naturally for everybody? Could flirting be taught?

I was fascinated by this subject, and I began to explore the secrets of successful flirting. I interviewed scores of people in and outside of the business world who also flirted successfully. I researched business theories that supported the notion that flirting works, and I examined achievements in my own life. I redefined flirting and created a seminar based on that data. Now, after several years of consulting, teaching, and speaking about these skills to Fortune 500 companies, I am thrilled to share with you how to gain success in business or any life situation. How to Flirt For Success.

Throughout my life I've been told "Jill, you have such a way with people." While such comments are flattering, they used to confuse me. Doesn't everybody act like this? I mean, the way I am with people — my flirting ability — just comes naturally. I've always known the benefits of feeling such affection and sharing it — people like and accept me, plus, it boosts their self-esteem. But several years ago I realized that flirting could also help me reach my goals and bring me success.

One particular incident, while not a goal-achieving moment, showed me how flirting could be helpful and, at the same time, make another person feel good. I was working on a late-night project with a co-worker. After three huge bowls of pretzels and three pitchers of soda, we finally finished the business proposal and left the restaurant. As I approached her neighborhood to drop her off, she gasped. "Jill, the speed limit here is only 25. You're going 45." Just then, of course, I noticed flashing lights behind me. My colleague shouted, "The police! We're going to get a ticket!" I remember thinking that this "being" who was stopping us was not just the "police" but a real, live person with feelings. Reminding myself I had people skills, I decided I could talk to this person just like I could talk to anyone else, and that if I acted scared, I would make things worse.

We pulled over. I had my license ready and I pulled the window down and gave a friendly "Hi." He asked me if I knew how fast I was going, and I calmly, but politely, told him the truth: I had never been in the area before and I just realized how fast I was going when he stopped me. He asked me to get out of the car. I willingly got out, smiled, and looked him in the eye. He asked me if I had been drinking. "No. Well, just a lot of Coca-Cola. And I ate a bunch of pretzels. Gosh, is my mouth salty." He laughed. Then I opened up a bit more. We had been working late ... we were exhausted ... I had never gotten a ticket before ... my workload was causing me to think less clearly. The more I talked, the more he laughed. I was upfront and friendly, and he was kind in return. With a smile he said he would let me go — just don't speed again.

When I got back in the car without a ticket, my associate was shocked. "Jill, how did you get out of that one?" At the time, I thought I treated the policeman like a human being and believed that he would respect me back. Today, I say I just flirted.

Anyway you look at it, I learned a useful concept: Before you label or stereotype people, give them and yourself a chance first by being genuine and expecting fairness. Now don't misunderstand me. I'm not advocating talking your way out of all tickets. What I am saying is that using fundamental flirting skills will give you the confidence to succeed in many situations. The more you try it, the easier it becomes.

I continued to flirt. A few years ago I interviewed for a position with a television talk show. My interview was at 10 a.m. I had never been to the studio, but I left in plenty of time and arrived plenty late — at 3:30. Yes, I drove two hours in the opposite direction. When I finally arrived, although nervous and frazzled, I looked the receptionist in the eye, called her by name (by reading her nameplate), and calmly though humorously told her about my faux-pas. "I'd really appreciate your help, Mrs. Green," I said after finishing my story. She smiled back and said. "It's Jane. Call me Jane. And I'll get you right in." I got the interview and I got the position. Best of all, I learned two valuable lessons: (1) Make sure you know where you're going, and (2) if you are sincere and warm, people will want to help you out. My "real life" education continued, and motivational speaking became my next goal.

The first place I tried to apply as a speaker initially turned me down, and rightly so. I sent them a sloppy application. They called to say they'd hold it on file, but I finally convinced them to meet with me for

a few minutes. I knew that if I could just get to
know them a little better, I could make a much more
positive impression. In person, I felt better. I had
the advantage of seeing the supervisor face-to-face
and I had ten full minutes to build rapport. At the
end of the interview they agreed to give me a try.
"Your application could be spruced up a bit, but
you're great in person and your enthusiasm will take
you far." Once again I learned that using good people skills — flirting — could save me in a less than
optimistic situation.

And now I have a published book, because I flirted. Three years ago a wonderful reporter, whom I
still feel indebted to, called me looking for some
information on a magazine article he was writing.
The article was about interesting classes offered in
the Twin Cities of Minneapolis and St. Paul. He had
read about my flirting class in a curriculum cata-
logue, and just needed to write a small blurb on it.
In ten minutes, I had given him the information he
wanted and he thanked me. But I was curious
about him. What else did he write about? Did he
write for other publications? After some flirting, he
told me he wrote for the main daily in town, *The Star
Tribune.* "Oh!" I began humbly, "you may want to do
a feature on me. I've got an interesting concept and
story to tell." He laughed at my enthusiasm (and
probably my nerve), and agreed to look at my press
kit. If he liked it, he would show it to his editor.

Three months later, I was featured on the cover of
the paper's Variety section with a picture and a full

color spread. I got more than 50 calls that day. And later in the week, I got calls from all over the country. The article had been syndicated nationally. But, the best call came from a publisher. He liked the story so much, he asked me to do this book. One conversation, one connection, had made all the difference. And it didn't cost me a thing, except the time investment it took to talk on the phone and the emotional investment it took to get to know someone else, which is a pay-off in itself.

In this book, you'll learn that success can be yours if you believe in yourself, appeal to people as kind human beings instead of preconceived stereotypes, and make sincere contact with others. Simply put, you'll learn how to flirt successfully.

For me, flirting has brought personal, professional, and financial success. And though it is second nature for me, I have learned by conducting flirting seminars that everyone can learn to flirt. We can learn so well, in fact, that it will begin to come naturally.

But before we go any further, we need to redefine flirting. Forget or put aside what you've known of flirting in the past. From now on, its definition is:

Building your self-esteem and the self-esteem in others by creating a warm, honest, and sincere rapport.

Based on this definition, you can flirt with every-body. This approach to flirting is not only fun, healthy, and fulfilling, it is also a way to develop lasting personal and professional success. Just think if all relationships were based on this type of rapport. They would be rooted in honesty and trust — the foundations that make relationships work and grow. And so while this book is not slanted toward romantic relationships, if all romantic attachments were based on this solid foundation, they would have a better chance of lasting fulfillment than those grounded on superficial aspects. So feel free to take what you learn here and bring it into a romantic arena. What we are focusing on in this book is learning to flirt to enhance lifetime people skills — something we all need as we deal with people every day.

Several years ago I worked for a direct sales com-pany and found it to be one of the most positive and beneficial experiences of my life. Everyone who worked there, from the president to the manager and the reps, were treated with fairness, encouragement, support, and respect. I started as a sales rep, and I remember my initial training seminar stressed the importance of treating the customer with an honest, serving, no-pressure approach. Why? Nobody wants to deal with, let alone buy from, someone they don't trust. When I moved into management, the same philosophy applied. We had management sem-inars on how to listen to, encourage, and support our sales reps. Unfortunately, too much of Corporate America uses negative reinforcement as a means to "control." The ideology behind my firm, however, focused on positive reinforcement. Our company motto became:

PEOPLE DON'T CARE HOW MUCH YOU KNOW UNTIL THEY KNOW HOW MUCH YOU CARE.

What a powerful concept, and one that is true. I applied this philosophy to my sales territory and I reached the number one position.

We all want to work for, with, or be surrounded by people who care for us as human beings and who have our best interests at heart. We know then we will be treated with respect. Therefore, we want to do the "best job" we can, whether we clean somebody's house, treat a patient, wait on a customer at a busy restaurant, or if we are one of the top managers of a Fortune 500 company.

Recently, Laura Polipnick, of Jack & Jill Foods, called me to do a seminar for her firm. She runs a chain of supermarkets with her son, and they wanted to give their managers a motivating weekend retreat. I was impressed by her style on the phone —very pleasant and warm. How refreshing to find a company owner so personable and so proud of her staff. "You'll be speaking to about 20 men. They're great guys, and we've never given them a conference like this before, so we really want to do something special for them," she told me.

When the date arrived, I was even more impressed with this woman and her staff upon meeting them in person. When I walked into the meeting room, there were 21 men sitting around the conference table, and one woman. She jumped up to greet me. Laura must have been in her early fifties but had the energy of a teenager, a sparkle in her eye, and an incredibly infectious smile. "We're so excited to have you join us, Jill," she said with enthusiasm. Her greeting made me feel so welcome, and I knew with her in charge, the morale of the staff would be positive.

Halfway through the seminar, we discussed how to turn a crisis into a learning experience. First, the staff shared their experiences in partners. Then I asked if anyone wanted to talk to the whole group. Usually, most people are reluctant, but Laura raised her hand right away. Her story was inspiring. "Well, the biggest crisis I've ever had happened a year ago when my husband, who used to own and run this company, died suddenly of a heart attack. I was a nurse at the time, and had been most of my life. My son Keith was just completing college and was planning to go to graduate school for business when my husband passed away. Keith and I thought long and hard about what to do. My husband loved his business and he would have been devastated if we just sold it. Plus, I thought his staff was great; I just couldn't abandon them. So, we decided to try to run the markets together. At least Keith knew a little about management from his courses, but I knew nothing. All I had was nursing training. But we put our minds to it and we did it! And look how well we're doing thanks to everyone's effort. What I learned from this crisis was how strong I can really be and that if you put your mind to anything, you can do it."

Laura's story explained a lot. No wonder her staff was so loyal. She ran the company like she nursed her patients, treating her employees with kindness, nurturing, dedication, and respect. Her nursing training was actually a major asset to her management skills. Wouldn't it be great if everyone would take a course or two in "bedside manner"?

At the end of the meeting many of the guys came up to me with some heartfelt feedback. One gentleman in particular liked the section on listening. He spoke at length about his sister who is a wonderful listener and how she has taught him a lot. When he walked away, Sharon approached me and whispered, "That's John. He's been with us the longest and he used to be so withdrawn. But ever since Keith and I took over, he has become so open. What a wonderful person." I added my two cents. "Laura, he has probably become so open thanks to you. Look at the example you set for your team. You're so willing to share and so dedicated, and you're also a fighter. We could use more role models like you." She blushed and accepted the compliment gracefully, but she refused to take all the credit and once again paid homage to her staff.

Laura's story is a classic example of positive management. It's not so much your technical skills that make you a successful manager, it's your attitude toward people and yourself. Laura truly cared about her staff, and, in turn, they wanted to make her proud. Conversely, if we work for, or are surrounded by, people who have no regard for anyone's interests but their own, we feel resentful and used. We often detach ourselves in such an environment to cope with these feelings.

That's exactly how another participant of one of my seminars described his workplace. Larry Jergen was an administrative and marketing assistant for a magazine publisher. He liked the industry but hated his boss. He was controlling and used his power to intimidate, Larry told me. "He never tells us when we do a good job, just when we do something wrong. Once he asked me to briefly research a topic for him to consider, since all the writers were too busy to check into it. I researched it heavily and ended up handing him a 10-page in-depth report. A few writers who saw it said it was good enough to submit as a story. But when I gave it to my boss, he didn't say a word — nothing. The next day he called me into his office only to ask me why I returned from my lunch break five minutes late. It was as if he had searched for something to criticize me about. I even asked him how he liked my report and he mumbled, 'fine.' And then he had the nerve to yell at me 'Be on time from now on' as I left his office."

Larry went on to cite numerous instances where his boss exerted this type of behavior. He confessed, "He just has to have every ounce of power. It's so insulting and it's so frustrating. The more he acts this way, the more I want to quit. I certainly don't want to give him any satisfaction by doing a decent job."

How many people can you think of who are in a similar situation right now? Perhaps you are? Do you dislike your boss or co-workers so much the job itself becomes a burden?

Fortunately, you can do a lot to influence your environment and relationships in general. As you read the following chapters, you'll learn how to show others you care by creating warm, honest, and sincere rapport. And when that happens, success will most likely follow. In an atmosphere where people care for one another, morale is higher, conflicts are resolved through healthy communication, and, as a result, productivity goes up. That's good business. That's flirting for success.

2

FLIRTING FUNDAMENTALS

FLIRTING:

Building your self-esteem and the self-esteem in others by creating a warm, honest, and sincere rapport.

Building a warm, honest, and sincere rapport seems to come easy with our best friends, our family, our mates, even our neighbors. So why can't we create this type of bond with everyone? The answer is simple, and complicated. The simple answer is that it takes hard work, concentration, and commitment to establish such a rapport with another person, and hard work never comes easy. The complicated part is that every human being is a complex animal with his or her own set of fears, doubts, and insecurities that can make even saying "Hi" to a stranger an enormously courageous task. The good news is that no matter how difficult flirting may seem, we are all capable of becoming expert flirts. Like any other skill, we can learn to build rapport.

Let's begin with the basics, what I call Flirting Fundamentals.

There are nine attributes we need to practice in order to build a sincere and warm rapport. Let's take an overview and then explore each point in depth. As you read each point, ask yourself do I practice these behaviors when dealing with people? If not, what is holding me back? Why do I exhibit such fundamentals with some people and not with others? The nine steps are:

1. EYE CONTACT
2. GOOD LISTENING
3. ASKING QUESTIONS
4. EXUDING CONFIDENCE
5. SHOWING HUMOR
6. BEING HONEST
7. LIKING AND RESPECTING PEOPLE
8. SHOWING A POSITIVE ATTITUDE, and
9. BEING AN ATTRACTIVE PERSON.

Now let's explore each point in depth.

Eye Contact. Most of us are familiar with the old adage, "The eyes are the window to the soul." It's true. Looking someone directly in the eye is one of the most intimate moments between two people. It's amazing how much we can feel about someone just by looking them in the eye. Warmth, enthusiasm, anger, anticipation, judgment (and the list goes on) can be conveyed in moments when we face each other eye-to-eye. We all have a certain degree of intuition which tells us about another person. And it is the eyes, first and foremost, that give us those clues.

Have you ever told a lie? Remember how difficult it was to give eye contact at that time? We knew that once we met the gaze of the other person, our eyes would express our guilt. Even when we don't tell the truth, our eyes will. As parents, we realize the power of eye-contact when dealing with our children. We gently command them, "Look me in the eye when you tell me you don't know who spilled on the carpet."

Conversely, we are more apt to trust someone who gives us that contact. But, it's not enough to just be able to look someone in the eye, we must do it with commitment. We've all had that discouraging experience of talking to someone who, for the most part, only seems to be listening. Oh, he might be sitting right across from us and saying all the comforting "uh-huhs" and "um-ums," but his eyes keep darting over our shoulder, or toward the door, or to someone else. Despite the body language and verbal assurances, his eyes say, "I'm not paying attention." We lose interest in keeping the conversation going.

So if you want to create instant interest with someone, look him or her right in eye. And if you want to keep that person interested in you, hold that eye contact strongly and directly.

One activity where eye contact is stressed is public speaking — eye contact is crucial in keeping an audience's attention. Many times I have felt that upon making eye contact with a certain individual in the audience, we have made a connection — a friendship. And after that initial eye-to-eye moment, that audience member rarely looks away. I can understand why. Once that connection has been made, a bond has been formed.

Suzanne Green of Highland Park, Illinois, who was making a presentation to a staff of 50, learned how eye contact could turn one indifferent listener into an enthusiast. She explained, "As I began my speech I noticed everyone in the room was paying attention, except for one gentleman who sat at a table in the back. During my introduction, he was looking out the window and seemed to be oblivious to the activity in the room. Every now and then he'd look at his watch or doodle on his notepad. He clearly gave the impression that he did not want to be there.

"As I began working the room with my eyes, I looked at him during one of his watch glances, and he looked up and caught me looking at him. We met eye-to-eye. For a moment he seemed uncomfortable, and then he relaxed. I looked at him in the eye a while longer and then I shifted to another person. When I made my rounds to the back of the room again, I expected this man to be back out the window, but he was still looking at me. Our eyes met again. I sensed warmth and interest from him and it continued throughout my speech. At the end of the presentation he approached me and said, `I have to admit, usually during these things I can't concentrate for a second. But you really got my attention and I was glad you did. Once I listened, I got some valuable information. Thank you.'"

Though it may seem simple, strong and direct eye contact is nonetheless a powerful tool in flirting.

A few years ago, at one of my sales seminars, I spoke to a man who had a similar story about the importance of eye contact. "Many years ago I sold burglar alarms," he said. "There was a salesman on our staff who had basically everything right. He looked professional, he was friendly, and he always knew what to say whether he was greeting somebody or negotiating. I admired his style, except one thing really hurt him. He just wouldn't look a person in the eye, but he did everything else so well. Anyway, eventually he had to quit — I think his lack of eye contact was causing him to lose sales. He was honest, he told customers the truth, but he didn't look at them straight on and it hurt him."

Yes, at times it can be difficult to hold strong, direct eye contact. There are many reasons why we may feel the need to look away during a one-to-one contact. We have already discussed one reason — deception. In order to remedy that, the answer is obvious — don't lie. Oprah Winfrey, who is celebrated for her honesty and "down-to-earth" style, brilliantly guided one of her guests into confession on

her show. This particular man was hiding something, and Oprah knew it. She saw him stare at the
floor while he spoke and never look his wife in the
eye. Finally, Oprah suggested, "Tell the truth. The
truth will set you free!" She was right. At her coax-
ing, he told the truth, and as he did he lifted his
head up and sat up straight. For the first time, he
looked his wife right in the eye and disclosed his
secret. The truth does set us free, and it keeps our
eye contact direct and our relationships honest.

Another reason for poor eye contact is low self-
esteem. When we feel poorly about ourselves, we
struggle to look in the eye of another because we
anticipate seeing judgment or scorn in that person's
eyes. Beth Sisken, a communications consultant,
once counseled a woman, Susan, who was terrified
to go on a job interview because she was afraid to
look at the interviewer. When Beth asked Susan
exactly what frightened her, she responded, "All I
have to do is look at the interviewer for a moment
and I know I'll see that she sees I'm not qualified."
Ironically, by building up this fear in her mind,
Susan was sabotaging her own chances of appearing
capable and trustworthy. Beth's advice to her
echoed the familiar cheer — fake it, till you make it.

Realizing it was too difficult for Susan to use
direct eye contact, Beth suggested she look at her
interviewer's eyebrows or nose bridge, which would
give the illusion of eye contact. Eventually, this
process would make it easier for Susan to slowly
shift her gaze to the eyes. Susan not only learned to

use eye contact effectively, but her self-esteem increased as she was able to present a more confident image.

This story shows us that we can learn and train ourselves to use strong, direct eye contact even if, for one reason or another, we are unaccustomed to such intimacy. Moreover, in addition to the self-esteem we gain from using eye contact, we also become better listeners. Looking someone in the eye helps us keep our full attention, both visual and audio, on the person with whom we are conversing — the person who deserves our attention. This notion of another person deserving our attention leads us into our next flirting fundamental — being a good listener.

Good Listening. When we truly listen to another person, we are giving them one of the greatest gifts — respect. As self-esteem expert Alan Zimmerman says, "In the moment of listening to another person, we are telling that individual that he or she is the most important person in the world to us." Think about it. Who in your life right now truly listens to you? They don't interrupt you. They give you their full attention. They make you feel that what you have to say is interesting and important. That's the person we most want to talk to. And that's what flirting is all about — making somebody feel valued.

In Dale Carnegie's successful book, *How to Win Friends and Influence People*, he tells of a dinner party where he met a distinguished botanist. Never having met a botanist before, Carnegie was fascinated and spent the whole night asking this expert questions about exotic plants and how to improve his own small garden. He even admits to ignoring the other guests so he could stay on the edge of the seat as the botanist spoke. When the night ended, Carnegie overheard his new acquaintance rave about Carnegie to the host, calling him stimulating and an extremely interesting conversationalist. To those remarks, Carnegie confesses, "An interesting conversationalist? Why, I had hardly said anything at all. But I had done this. I had listened intently. And he felt it. That kind of listening is one of the highest compliments we can pay to anyone." And that's just how we feel when someone listens to us.

I don't think I've ever worked harder in my life than when I was a branch manager for a sales firm. When I look back on what motivated me, there was a strong heartfelt feeling that made me work. More than money or recognition, I wanted to make my supervisor proud. Marty Domitrovich was his name. When we first met, I was shocked at how quiet and calm he was. For some reason I expected someone more outspoken and intimidating. Marty was just the opposite. Instead of telling us how he moved up the ranks, he was more interested in our personal interests and our long term goals, and how and if our lives were balanced. Instead of talking about himself, Marty would much rather listen to us. Through his dedication to hear us out and understand our needs, Marty showed he truly cared about our well-being. In turn, we truly cared about his well-being, his success, and his long-term goals.

Just by taking the time to listen to his managing team as individuals, he created the most committed, driven, and loyal group of managers in the entire firm; a group that became the firm's top performing team. Because he listened, we no longer just wanted to produce for ourselves; we also wanted to produce for Marty. Does that mean Marty was an expert flirt? According to our definition — absolutely! Marty built a warm, honest, and sincere rapport by spending most of his time listening. We all want to feel appreciated and feel that we are interesting to others. Listening is a great way to show that.

But listening isn't easy. Listening takes a tremendous amount of dedication, concentration, and commitment. In fact, studies say that we use only 25% of our inherent listening ability. This makes sense. Think about all the interruptions there are at the office and at home — ringing phones, nearby conversations, knocks at the door — it's easy to get distracted. But in the moment that someone gets distracted away from us, we feel isolation.

Has anyone just stopped looking at you while you were telling a story, or interrupted you to talk to someone else? Maybe they were just "spacing out" as my young cousin says. Intentional or not, when people don't listen, we feel bad. Eleven-year-old Zoe Stern advises parents in her book, *Questions Kids Wish They Could Ask Their Parents*, to listen. "When parents don't listen or act like they're listening when they're doing two things at once, kids feel hurt." Fortunately, when we do use our listening skills, we increase the confidence of others.

Because listening is such a critical element to flirting and difficult to do, we will examine it in greater depth in Chapter 4. For now, let's continue our discussion of fundamentals by examining one of the most outstanding traits of a good listener — ASKING QUESTIONS.

Asking Questions. Remember the motto, PEOPLE DON'T CARE HOW MUCH YOU KNOW UNTIL THEY KNOW HOW MUCH YOU CARE? Well, asking questions is one of the best ways to show that you care and it takes listening a step further. When we ask people questions about themselves, their interests, their opinions, we make people feel appreciated and special. Can you think of anyone who doesn't want to feel like that?

It's like a first date. You know, that exciting time when we literally feel like we are being interviewed by our companion and that we are in an audition. Where are you from? What do you do? Do you enjoy your work? What are your hobbies? Etc. What's the motivation behind these questions? To build rapport. To find what we have in common with this individual. And the more we find we have in common, the more intimate or connected we feel. There is a sense of joy in finding out we both love to ski, we both enjoy the same author, we both are the youngest in our families. Of course, it's impossible to have everything in common with someone else, but in that fact there's also a thrill. Learning we have differences offers us the opportunity to teach each other something new.

Moreover, on first dates people tend to give 100%. We work hard to get to know the person, and they work hard to make a favorable impression. Well, imagine the type of rapport you would build if you applied these techniques to everyone you met. Now I'm not suggesting that you "date" them literally. But take the effort to ask probing questions that show you care and make an equal effort to be yourself and make a positive impression.

Kyle Burchord, a videographer, told me about a project that required the assistance of a lawyer, named Stu. When they first met, Stu was "all business" and immediately started to discuss contracts. Of course, Kyle could have followed his lead and attended to business right away. However, knowing that he may be consulting this lawyer many times during the project, Kyle decided it was important to build a comfortable, trusting rapport that would enhance their business endeavors. He decided to "flirt."

Kyle asked Stu questions that showed he was interested in him as a person. He asked how long he had been a lawyer and what he liked most about it, where he went to school, what led him into the field, if he saw this as a lifetime career or had other aspirations.

As he listened to the explanations, Kyle noticed Stu's demeanor had changed; he seemed to become more enthusiastic and relaxed as their conversation progressed, and the tone of the meeting grew from

tension to enjoyment. And after Stu had the "spot-
light," he began returning the interest by asking Kyle
probing questions along the same lines. What was
Kyle's background, his favorite part about his job,
his long-term goals? By first asking questions, Kyle
created an openness. And even though their scheduled session was coming to a close, Stu said Kyle
could stay until all of his questions were answered.
Because Kyle had taken the initiative to build a
warm rapport, his lawyer wanted to do his best job
for Kyle regardless of the extra time. Once their
business relationship had a friendship quality, the
work itself was much more enjoyable. In fact, after
just one meeting, the lawyer referred two clients to
Kyle whom he thought might want Kyle's services.
And it all happened because Kyle had decided to
flirt.

Political analysts and others were deeply impressed with President Clinton's style at his pre-elec-
tion town meetings. He seemed to have a special
ability of connecting with the audience and making
them feel understood. How so? By asking questions. Once a man stood up and said, "How can you
understand the recession when you and everyone
else around you still have their jobs?" Clinton
responded by asking, "Have you lost your job?" The
man seemed surprised and responded, "Yes."
Clinton went on, "Have your friends and others
around you also lost theirs?" The man quietly
answered "yes" again. Clinton paused, expressed
sincere empathy, and then explained his plan for the
economy. Everyone was ready to listen because, by

asking this man questions, Clinton had captured our attention. He had reached out to a common citizen and made him feel important, valued, and human.

Asking questions is also a useful tool when being interviewed for a job. Every question an interviewer asks is done to see if you are qualified for the position. In those questions, the interviewer leads the discussion, evaluates us, and controls the meeting. What would happen if you asked questions back when the interviewer was through? After all, you want to make sure the company is right for you. Ask interviewers what they like about their job. Or what they like best about the company's atmosphere. Those types of questions show that you, too, want to see if the company is "well-suited for you." Not only do you have the right to, but it makes sense. It's a big decision on everyone's part.

I recently met a human resources manager for a large insurance company. He had interviewed hundreds of people over his career. When I asked him what made the best interviews, he said, "Usually when they interview me." He spoke of one gentleman in particular who seemed fairly reserved during the first half of the interview. "There wasn't much about him that stood out until I asked him, 'Do you want to ask me anything?' At that point, he took out a list and asked some of the most thoughtful and intelligent questions I had heard in awhile." I was very impressed with him after that.

Good flirts also try to ask questions that require in-depth answers, not one word answers. The key is to stay away from Yes or No set-ups. Notice the difference:

Do you like your job?
>Yes/No
>**BETTER**: What specifically do you like about your job?

Do you like the morale here?
>Yes/No
>**BETTER**: How would you describe the morale here?

Do you think I have a good chance of being hired?
>Yes/No
>**BETTER**: What do you need to see from me in order to get hired here?

By asking open-ended questions we build healthy, trusting relationships. We show people that we care enough to take the time to "find out more" and that we respect others enough to listen to their opinions. Of course, in certain situations, we don't have time to ask a lot of questions. Yet, even a simple, "Are you having a rough day?" to an overworked waiter can create a more trusting, relaxed atmosphere in addition to bringing you better service.

Sandra Dubrow, a stockbroker for a Chicago firm, wanted to impress some potential clients so she took them to lunch at one of the most expensive, and crowded, restaurants in town. Her party was seated immediately, but their service went downhill from there. The waiter was overworked with six full tables. Apparently, all of his tables felt they were receiving poor service. "Hurry up with our food. We've got to go soon!" one customer snapped. Another customer called the manager over to complain, "We need to make a meeting. This is ridiculous!" Sandra felt the aggression in the room build, and she even noticed that her clients were perturbed by the slow service. None of the negative comments seemed to be improving the situation, so Sandra decided to try a different philosophy. When the waiter finally arrived with the meals, Sandra joked, "What a day you must be having. Do they include juggling in your training?" The waiter laughed and replied, "Thanks for understanding." Service from then on seemed to pick up. The waiter stopped by their table several times. He also served free desserts to apologize for the earlier slow service. The food was excellent, the meal ended on time, and her clients left in a good mood. Just by putting herself in the waiter's shoes and treating him with kindness, Sandra turned adequate service into exceptional results.

Exuding Confidence. So far, we have discussed three fundamentals that will enhance your communication with others: looking them in the eye, being a good listener, and asking questions. All these activities make people feel good about themselves. And the more we can help others like themselves, the more they will like us. However, making others feel good about themselves is only a part of reciprocal admiration. Good flirts also know that even before we make that eye contact and before we ask questions, we need to exude a certain amount of confidence that will make others want to be around us in the first place. People want to work or deal with individuals who have confidence. The more you believe in yourself, the more others believe in you. So, conversely, if you don't show belief in yourself, then you may have trouble finding people who will. Confidence attracts, inspires, and motivates others.

Several years ago I spoke with the recruiting manager of an international marketing firm who learned the power of confidence through his job. He would present information about the company to groups of 20 people. He spent a great deal of time explaining the unlimited pay plan and showing the outstanding program, both of which he truly believed in. After a session he would ask each applicant why he or she wanted to work with the firm. "The one I remember the most was a young man who said, 'Because I want to be as happy in my job as you are in yours.'"

The confidence the manager projected in himself and his firm out-measured anything he could have said about the benefits, the product, or even money. In fact, people pay more attention to the confident image you exude than the words you say or the tone of your voice.

Sixty percent of communication is non-verbal, which means people form opinions about us based on what they see — how we carry ourselves, dress, and use facial expressions — more than what we say. That being the case, an important strategy to use is to try to appear at our most confident at all times. Even if we're nervous. Remember the commercial that said, "Never let 'em see you sweat." When you want to make a positive impression, carry yourself in such a way that shows you are worth believing in! So, if you need to "fake it till you make it," that's okay. Put your shoulders back, head up high, look people in the eye, and "play" confident. In no time at all you'll feel empowered.

A woman once asked me how she could improve her ability to enjoy new situations like parties or network meetings. She said she always felt alone at new gatherings. After seeing her at a function, it wasn't difficult to see why. She walked into the room, glanced at people, then looked away, avoided all groups, and found a comfortable place to stand by and wait. You can see the signal she was sending to others: Don't approach me, I feel closed.

I just spoke with this woman recently and was delighted to hear she's now having a ball at gatherings. "I'm a hit!" she exclaimed. She went on to say that now when she enters a room of strangers, she walks to the center of the room, stands confidently, looks passersby in the eye with a smile, and before she knows it, she's got a crowd around her.

The history of the world is full of men who rose to leadership by sheer force of self-confidence, bravery, and tenacity.
— Mahatma Gandhi

Confidence and belief are exactly what Steven Parker needed to get his multi-million dollar business started. He grew up in poverty and received a poor education. But he had ambition and desire to get out of his neighborhood. "I'm going to make something of myself," he told himself everyday. He knew that all he had to do was learn a trade, and from there he could create a business. So he learned to lay tile. He learned every facet and theory about the tile business. And when he felt he knew all there was to learn, he set out to start his own tile kingdom.

With no capital, and few business contacts, Steven's only resort was to get a bank loan. He knew that if he could just get the bank to believe in him, he could have that money and pursue his dream. Before he left for the bank, he took two hours to get ready. He put on his best shirt, which at the time was a plain white t-shirt. He borrowed a pair of jeans from his brother, because all of his were torn. And he tied his long hair back in a neat pony-tail after shaving his face. "I'm going to get that loan," he declared to the mirror. The loan officer was pleasant and seemed to know his job. After asking Steven a series of questions, he explained how the bank was very selective in its loans and he didn't think he could approve Steven's loan request.

"I'll tell you why I should get that loan," Steven began with pride and conviction. He looked the loan officer straight in the eye, leaned in, pierced his eye-brows and said, "Because I'm going to make something of myself. I'm going to have a great business. I'm going to make a lot of money. I'm going to like what I do. And, I'm going to give back to my community. That's why." The loan officer was silent. "O.K., young man. I'll take a chance on you. You can have that loan." When the loan officer told me that story, he explained that Steven had one quality that stood out from any other loan applicant he had ever met. "He had a confidence and determination like none I had ever seen! He made me believe in him. I couldn't help but believe in him."

Self-confidence is a vital flirting fundamental, but it's hard to maintain day after day. There is an old expression that begins: "To err is human." I think the second half to that quip should be: "To beat yourself about it, even more human." In Chapter 3 we will take an in-depth look at the power of self-confidence and how to create and maintain it on a daily basis. Speaking of maintenance, one of the best ways to maintain a sense of personal esteem, balance, or even sanity is to have a sense of humor — our next fundamental.

Showing Humor. Johnny Carson once said, "People will pay more money to be entertained than educated." Think about it. We would rather deal with people who have a sense of humor than those who take everything so seriously. Humor helps to create a sense of ease, which is essential in the world of flirting. When we share a laugh with someone else, we feel more comfortable and connected with them. In fact, while having a sense of humor on one level feels (in the most basic of definitions) "fun", it is a large factor in mental health and personal success and an enormous link to recovery.

In Norman Cousin's book, *Anatomy of An Illness*, he says humor therapy was used to cure a form of spinal disease. How did they do it? A consistent diet of funny movies and re-runs of TV's comical "Candid Camera."

Furthermore, the creator of the Comedy Cart Program, which provides humor stimulation for hospital patients, said in a recent article that laughter is a stress reducer, releasing us from tension and pent-up feelings. Moreover, she says a well-developed sense of humor "can preserve our self-respect and protect us from self-pity. When we poke fun at the tension areas in our lives, we are better prepared to deal with them. And if we can laugh at ourselves first, other people will find it difficult to laugh at us." Taking this last comment a step further, when we laugh at ourselves first, we also invite others around us to laugh at themselves — and in that, we express to others that it is o.k. to make mistakes. In fact, it is "human."

Realizing that humor is an integral part of "flirting" may make some people uncomfortable. During one of my seminars on the subject, a participant raised his hand and said, "What do you do if you're not funny?" I asked him to elaborate on what "being funny" means. He made references to the kind of people who are always "cracking jokes" and have the ability to come up with "quick lines." Well, I had good news for him — a sense of humor shows up in many different ways other than just cracking jokes and exhibiting a flair for comebacks.

In fact, one of the best ways to show how funny you are is by enjoying other people's jokes. I have a colleague named Laura Perry who, in addition to being so much fun to be around, is also one of the funniest people I've ever met. When we're together, I can barely stop laughing. Surprisingly, Laura doesn't talk that much. In fact, she barely sneaks a word in edgewise. And the reason I'm convinced she is one of the funniest people I've ever met is because she laughs at everything I say. In other words, I think Laura has such a great sense of humor because she is able to fully enjoy mine. And that makes her a person with whom I *want* to work.

In addition to laughing at other's jokes, there are other ways to show we have a sense of humor. Finding something humorous in every situation is one way of expressing humor. Jenna Sandler told me about her father who has a wonderful ability of doing this. "When I was very young, my family and I would join other families on the Fourth of July at a park for spectacular fireworks. One year the weather was so bad and the sky so cloudy that we couldn't see the fireworks, we could only hear them. Everybody was either sulking or complaining about this unfortunate condition, except my father. Every time he'd hear the bang of a firecracker bursting, he'd point to the sky and say, 'Wow! Look at that one!' or 'Jenna, look at those colors.' Our family and friends started giggling as he continued with his charade, sometimes exaggerating his act with, 'Look out! It's falling straight toward us.' And sometimes he'd be a little sarcastic, 'I haven't had this much fun since the time we couldn't even see the fireworks.' Soon we were laughing so hard, we began to draw attention to ourselves. Many other families wanted to know what was so funny about overcast fireworks. After watching my dad for awhile, they started laughing, too. Before we knew it, people were moving their blankets toward us and even joining in on the antics. Kids were tugging on their parent's sleeves, "That one is the best!" and parents were smiling, delighting in this fantasy. By the finale, we had all laughed until our stomachs ached, and we also made some wonderful new friends. Everyone agreed it was the best Fourth of July ever. And it all began because my father was able to take a disappointing situation and find the humor in it."

Twenty years after the fireworks incident, Jenna used the same strategy. As the head of an advertising agency, Jenna set up a private screening for a potential client to show some of her firm's best commercials. Jenna, her assistant, and the five visiting executives waited for the film to begin in the small screening room. A few people coughed uncomfortably when the screen remained dark several minutes after Jenna's introduction. She remembered her father that Fourth of July. "I just love the spokesperson in this one," Jenna said out loud. "She's so

subtle. You can't even tell she's selling you anything." Everyone laughed at her remark. "Yes," said
one visiting executive, "your firm uses an interesting
visual style. Blank is the only way to go." More
laughs rose until everyone spoke up trying to top the
last clever remark.

Simply looking at the bright side of a situation is
another way to show humor. A door-to-door sales
rep I met was great at taking a seemingly hopeless
situation and finding a bright side. Once a woman
opened her door in anger, screamed, "I don't want
any!" and slammed the door in his face. At that
point he said to himself that it couldn't get any
worse, so he might as well try one more time. So, he
went to the back door, knocked again, and this time
when the same woman answered, he said, "Gosh. I
hope you're a lot nicer than the angry woman who
answered the front door." This time he got her to
laugh and take a look at herself. She let him in and
he made the sale.

A social worker told me how he used humor to
keep his job. After several staff members were continually late to work, his boss warned everyone that
if they were more than 10 minutes late, they'd be
dismissed. A week later, this particular man was 15
minutes late. Boldly, he walked into his boss' office
and asked for a job application. When his boss
asked why, he responded, "Well, according to my
watch, there is a recent opening." His boss laughed
and told him to get to work. Thanks to a good sense
of humor, the application wasn't necessary.

Laughing at ourselves is also a way of showing humor and flirting. I had to laugh at myself during a "speaking club" meeting I attended several months ago. I am a member of Toastmasters, an organization that focuses on speech communication. I know the club members very well, and truly look forward to our weekly meetings. However, in this one particular meeting, I was not in my usual positive frame of mind. It was one of "those days." You know, the kind where: the alarm went off at the wrong time, I couldn't find my shoes, I had a stubborn hair bump, my car wouldn't start, etc. By the time I arrived at the meeting, I was 15 minutes late. I quietly snuck in and braced myself. All I had to do was learn the theme of the day, adjust my talk to it, and everything would be fine.

The day's theme is always written on a piece of paper and placed on our chairs. That day the theme happened to be Positive Mental Attitude. On the paper it simply said "P.M.A." Well, keep in mind how distorted I felt that day. I looked down and saw P.M.S.! At first, I felt confused. But when I looked back up at the speaker, who was engrossed in explaining a microchip in words I couldn't understand, I was convinced P.M.S. was our theme. So, after I was introduced, I held my chin high, my shoulders back, smiled, made eye contact, and began my talk. "Thank you club members. In keeping with the theme of P.M.S., I would like to . . ." At that moment, everyone gasped and looked at each other. Sensing my faux-pas, I checked the theme one more time and saw my grave error. As the room was still haunted in silence, I thought about what I had done and began to laugh. Pretty soon everyone else was laughing too. I'm sure they all wanted to burst out initially, but it was my self-mockery that invited them to also poke fun with me. In this case, I showed my humorous side without being clever, cracking a joke, or even thinking up something quick.

We can all show how funny we are if we just learn to look at things a little differently. And that brings me to a very comforting point — humor can be acquired. You can train yourself to look at the bright side, find the humor in situations and laugh at yourself and the irony in the world. When I feel down, in fact, I have found my best medicine is to plant myself in front of my TV, watch the comedy channel, and just laugh until I feel better. Everyone loves to laugh and we love to be around people who make us laugh. Good flirts laugh a lot.

Being Honest. Our next flirting fundamental lays the groundwork for all lasting and trusting relationships. It is, in fact, written right into our new definition of flirting. Since we have defined flirting as creating a warm, honest, and sincere rapport, then honesty is vital in establishing and maintaining healthy relationships. Common sense tells us that people want to deal with honest people and don't want to deal with people whom are seen as dishonest. In his book, *Swim With the Sharks Without Being Eaten Alive*, Harvey Mackay writes, "The most important term in any contract isn't the contract.

It's dealing with people who are honest." Unlike some of the other fundamentals we have discussed so far such as eye contact or good listening, honesty is not necessarily a concept that we can learn in a book or seminar; it is more of a personal decision.

Everyone makes a conscious choice to either live in integrity or not. Sounds simple, but actually it is not. Being honest can be a struggle — from truthfully telling someone you dislike their haircut, to showing up for a meeting exactly at the time you said you would, to being honest enough to show your true self instead of hiding behind a false facade. Indeed, we show we are honest in many ways. The first way is simply telling the truth.

Certainly, we all want to be truthful because we want to feel good about ourselves and we want others to trust and like us. We also want honesty from others in return. Yet, sometimes telling the truth is difficult; excuses seem much easier or can seem to get us "off the hook." We all know the old story about the student who pretends that the dog ate his homework.

Even as adults, we make up excuses. One woman shared her experience with me while we were discussing the notion of "white lies" during an ethics conference. "A colleague of mine gave a small dinner party last week and served one of the best sponge cakes I, and some of the guests (according to their comments), had ever eaten. We raved about this treat and asked her for the recipe. Blushing, she refused, telling us it was an old family secret. After all the guests had left, I stayed to help clean-up. While we were alone doing the dishes, I said to my friend, 'Come on. You can tell me.' With her head and eyes down and a look of extreme guilt, she said, 'O.K. The recipe is in there,' and pointed to the trash basket. Resting on top was an empty Sarah Lee tin. 'I was too embarrassed to tell them I didn't make it myself,' my friend confessed. Since that party, she has asked me several times if I still respect her. Perhaps that's a question she should be asking herself."

The worst and perhaps most harmful thing that happens to us when we lie is that we lose the respect we have for ourselves. When that happens, it is nearly impossible to expect respect from others. The truth is always better. A recent sales article said 75% of dissatisfied customers will do business again with a company that admits its mistakes and corrects them.

One sales trainer told me she made more sales when she was truthful about not having the answers than when she talked her way around tough questions. She recalled, "I made two sales calls in a row one day with different approaches on each, and the results surprised me. I felt uptight on my first appointment that day because I was dealing with a very well-known woman in the business community. A few of her questions stumped me, but I'd say, 'I think so,' even though I wasn't sure. She seemed to enjoy my presentation, but I didn't get the sale. On my next presentation, I went through my pitch exactly the same. The only difference was when I was asked questions I didn't know, I responded, 'Actually, I really don't know, but I can check.' I left that customer with a smile on my face and a sales agreement in my hand. I later asked that customer what he liked best about my presentation. He told me it was my honesty; that I didn't pretend to know the answers."

Not pretending or just "being yourself" is another way to express your honesty. In fact, one of our best assets is showing our vulnerable side or our "real self" to others.

In the movie "Beaches," Bette Midler brilliantly exposes her vulnerable side in one of the picture's most memorable scenes. During the course of the film, Bette's character becomes a big movie star. And in this particular scene, one of her long-time friends, along with her husband, pays Bette a visit to catch up on lost time. Bette's character has become a commercial success, but she still has a quality of insecurity and talks about her success incessantly. Her company grows more embarrassed as Bette takes her friends up to her flamboyantly decorated apartment and explains how much it costs. After her lengthy monologue, Bette finally pauses, turns to her guests and says, "Enough about me. Let's talk about you. What do you think of me?" and she follows her comment with a blush and a giggle. Up to this point, Bette's overzealousness to impress her guests makes them feel awkward, just as we all feel when others are "putting on a show." Yet, with that one line, she endears us to her because she is self-mocking, vulnerable, and openly admits her insecurity. Now that her character has shown her "true self," we like her more. Indeed, honesty is always the best policy, and part of that policy is being yourself.

The final way in which we show others we are honest, in addition to telling the truth and being ourselves, is keeping our word. How many of us routinely get to appointments or meetings 10 minutes late? How many times do we say to a friend, "I'll call you tomorrow" and never do? Isn't it easy to just say, "Let's have lunch," even though we don't really mean it? At one time or another we all have done such things, but have we stopped to take a look at the kind of message we are sending to others? When we're late for a lunch date, for example, the message we are sending to our companion is, "Your time, and even you, are not important enough for me to arrive on time. My time is more important." When we tell someone we'll call tomorrow and don't, the message we send is, "I really didn't mean it. I don't care enough to remember to call you." Even when we spew, "Let's do lunch," but never make the attempt to do it, we appear insincere. And while we may rationalize and tell ourselves, "Oh, they won't care if I'm late or forget to call," in actuality, people are hurt by this type of behavior and take emotional notes on our insincerity, often losing a great deal of trust and faith in us.

Think about how you feel when others don't keep their word. Honesty and integrity are about personal commitment. Everyone has the freedom to choose an honest value system and decide if they want to live by their word. So, if you want to be an effective flirt and gain the respect of others, start by respecting yourself — tell the truth, be yourself, and live by your word.

Liking and Respecting People. We have just spent some time examining the concept of liking and respecting ourselves. Liking yourself is important because it is the first step to others liking and respecting you as well — something everyone needs and a crucial part to personal success. Another way to ensure others will like and respect you is by liking and respecting them. I overheard two children express this concept beautifully one day in a restaurant. A young girl asked her older sister for her extra cookie. "O.K., but can I have your chips?" "No!" screamed the little girl. Her older sister then retorted, "Denise, you have to give if you want to get!" Words of wisdom.

In the world of people skills, good flirts know the importance of liking and respecting *all* people. Conversely, people who live in judgment of others tend to be very poor flirts. Take a moment and ask yourself, "Why would I want to be so willing to make contact with others? Here is the answer: EVERYONE IS AN OPPORTUNITY. In the business world, this concept is called networking. The idea: The more people you meet, the more you increase your chances to get business. And if you do not get business from them directly, they may lead you to someone who does.

Arnold Stone runs a small but profitable insurance agency. He's had the same five employees working for him over 10 years. He explained to me one day how he met each of them. "That's Freda. She used to babysit my kids. She was always reliable, friendly, and resourceful. When I needed a good secretary, my wife reminded me about her. The kids were grown and I hadn't seen Freda for years, but I gave her a call. She's as professional here as I remember then. That's Steven. I went to college with his sister's husband. I met Steven at their wedding. He made a great impression from the start. That's Joan. Her neighbor answered an ad we placed in the paper. She didn't want the job, but she knew someone who would — Joan. That's Tom. His uncle was my mechanic for years. He always bragged about his talented nephew. He was right. And that's Kate. She lives in the same apartment building as my dentist's son. I was getting my teeth cleaned one day and mentioned to my dentist that I needed a good organizer who could work computers. He checked around and found us Kate."

Does Arnold's story sound familiar? If we took the time to trace back how various people led us to other people or to other opportunities, we would discover some fascinating paths to the road of success. Networking is not only necessary, it is natural: People want to help other people.

Now, at this point, I need to make sure I am not misunderstood. When I say everyone is an opportunity, I don't mean just to improve business or enhance a social life. In fact, in order for clarification, I should expand this phrase into EVERYONE IS AN OPPORTUNITY TO LEARN. To learn what, you may ask. To learn about everything! To learn more about yourself, to learn about them, to learn about the world, to learn anything and everything. Let's take a look at some examples.

A well-known actor in Hollywood desperately wanted to get a certain film made. He had almost everything he needed: A script that he believed in, a group of talented actors who wanted to be in the film, he even had the necessary production staff. There was one problem, however — no studio would back the project. And that one problem kept the film from being made. The project lay stagnant for months. The actor just couldn't get the financial backing he needed. But then came a surprise. One day the actor was looking for cars at a prominent dealership when he ran into the owner. The owner recognized the actor and struck up a conversation. The two men talked at length and the actor spoke about his struggle over the project. "It sounds like it would make a great film. Can I read the script?" the owner asked. The actor was surprised but nonetheless flattered and decided no harm could come from this. He agreed to share the script. One week later, the actor received a phone call from the dealership owner. "I love the script, and I really think it could be a blockbuster. I'd like to finance the project."

Just by striking up a conversation with a stranger, two men changed their lives. When you like and respect people, you reach out and open our lives up to amazing possibilities.

Two years ago I had a seminar to give and arrived 30 minutes early to prepare. As I arranged my notes, the only other person in the room was a janitor who was setting up chairs. Engrossed in my preparation, I didn't even think of saying Hi. Well, I certainly learned my lesson. He noticed I was shuffling my papers and heard me mumble that I hoped everything would go well. "Ma'am, I don't know what you're so worked up about! This thing tonight will go great, and you'll be great. They're going to love you, so just relax and believe in yourself."

Well, to my own shock, I was so motivated by this spirited gentleman that I would have much rather sat in the audience and taken a seminar from him. If everyone is an opportunity to learn, then I learned a great deal from this man. I learned that when I block out people, I may be missing an opportunity. He was just the boost I needed to make the seminar a success. And I learned that you should never assume that you can't learn from everyone. I was supposed to be the motivator in the room and here was the janitor motivating me.

Another time I was sitting alone at an airport, waiting to board a plane. Two teenagers were sitting near me so I struck up a conversation with them. We chatted for awhile about college and life in general, and I told them about my profession and gave them a business card. We talked for about 10 minutes before boarding the plane and sitting in different sections.

Two months later, I got a call. These same two teenagers wanted me to send my press kit to the dean of their school in hopes that their university would hire me to speak. A week later, another call came and I was flown out to North Dakota and back for a very nice sum. It was my first out-of-state booking all because I struck up a conversation with two teenagers at an airport.

So what is the lesson here? People you haven't met yet aren't "strangers" — they're opportunities! It is amazing how one conversation can lead to so many things. And that goes beyond speaking with a new person. If you have an idea you want to market, or are looking for an opportunity, let everyone know. Some of your own friends, or their friends, may have the answer.

Take Coleen Fouler, for example. Her son, Michael, was given a special present by his best friend Ryan. It was a handmade book about two different flavored ice cream cones becoming friends. (Michael and Ryan are of different ethnic backgrounds.) Coleen was so impressed with the story, pictures, and message, that she casually mentioned the book to a friend who worked at a chemical dependency clinic. He thought it was a great idea and suggested she talk to a director on the clinic's

Board who had worked for a toy manufacturer.
Coleen called him and today she is the proud publisher of the acclaimed children's book series
"Double Scoop." You never know. Talk to everybody.

Showing A Positive Attitude. Just like deciding
to live honestly and opening our minds to liking all
kinds of people (our previous two fundamentals), our
next fundamental is also about attitude. Good flirts
are positive. People like to feel good and want to be
around positive people. Think about the people in
your life who are very positive. How do they express
their uplifting outlooks? Is it just through language?
Or do they also show their positive outlooks by the
way they carry themselves, their aura, the way in
which they live their lives?

I once did some personal consulting for a gentleman from a financial firm who wanted to work on
his image. At our first meeting I asked him various
questions including how he felt he came across to
other people and how he'd like to come across to
people. He said, "I'd like to make the type of impression Louie does, who works here at the firm." After
asking, what kind of impression Louie makes, my
client responded, "Well, it's hard to explain. You'd
have to meet him. He's just, well, a great guy.
Everybody likes Louie." I went on to ask him for
Louie's last name and what department he worked
in. "Actually, I'm not sure," my client said, "but you
have to meet him. He's such a great guy."

Fortunately, the company was having an office party that week and I accompanied my client. I was anxious to meet this Louie. My client and I were some of the first people to arrive at the party. As we walked into the room, my associate looked around and whispered to me, "He's not here yet." My curiosity was building as I kept one eye on the door to see if he had come yet. I had conjured up an image of a tall man who spoke with charisma and had an obvious star quality about him. "That's Louie!" my partner nudged me. When I turned to look, I found myself surprised. Louie was short and seemed to blend in with the group of people he came in with. "That's him?" I thought. But suddenly, at closer look, I too could tell something was special about this Louie. First of all, he walked with ease and grace — he almost flowed into the room. He had a youthful face, except for extreme wrinkles just around his eyes, apparently from perpetual smiling. I don't remember him speaking to anyone when he arrived, but he was laughing a lot and shaking hands and making eye contact with everyone. And his eyes were always sparkling. He worked the room, wandering from one cluster of people to another. "Hey, Lou!" people kept acknowledging. He'd join a crowd for a while, adding his sparkle, laughing and shaking hands, and then he'd move on. Finally, my partner introduced Louie to me.

As I stood close to Louie, I could feel warmth radiating from him, from the twinkle in his eyes to the sincerity of his firm but gentle handshake. All he said was, "Nice to meet you," but I liked him immedi-

ately. I watched him throughout the party and I
don't remember him saying much at all. But, it
didn't matter. Apparently, everyone felt this way
about Louie. His name kept coming up as one of the
greatest people in the firm, and yet I don't recall
anyone mentioning his last name or even the department he worked in. And yet, he was one of the most
popular people in the company.

After the party, my client and I were walking back
to our cars, "See what I mean? Can you teach me to
have that Louie quality?" What made Louie such a
great guy was not particularly what he said or did, it
was the way he made people feel. His aura was one
of warmth and genuineness, and he had spirit that
uplifted everyone around him. Just by the way he
carried himself, Louie was a positive person. And
everyone felt more positive when he was around.

The more sincerely positive our behavior, the more
others have faith in us. In addition to our behavior,
aspects of our language can also express our optimistic outlook. That doesn't mean we need to go
around claiming how great our life is, how wonderful
our day is, etc. But we need to pay attention to the
subtle messages we send to others. Top sales train-
ers realize this important idea when they teach the
dos and don'ts of customer satisfaction. And that
satisfaction begins way before a product is used.

Don't ever leave a customer with the words, "I
hope you like it!" The word "hope" connotes
doubt. Customers remember those last words and

subconsciously repeat them in their minds. "Um I hope I like it ..." which eventually evolves into, "Gosh, I hope I like it. Will I like it? Maybe I won't. I hope I did the right thing. I could return it and think about it." *Do* leave a customer with, "I know you're going to love it." The word "know" connotates faith and belief. These words evolve into, "I know I'm going to love it. I do love it. I did the right thing. Maybe I'll buy more."

Take this philosophy and apply it to managing people. As a supervisor, would you want to tell your employee, "Good luck on the assignment. I hope you can do it" or "I know you're going to do a great job on this assignment. I believe in you."? Which statement is the best motivator? When we tell our children we know they'll do well on their test, we instill much more confidence than when we tell them we hope they do well.

Other language subtleties exist in the acceptance of compliments. When we graciously accept a compliment with a sincere "thank you," we show our positive side versus disagreeing with someone's kind comment, which shows negativity and often hurts them. Have you ever told a co-worker you really liked her presentation and she responded with, "Really? I think I could have slowed down." Instead of refuting compliments, we need to return kind words with something like, "Thanks. That makes me feel good," to show how positively we can receive comments. (More on complimenting in Chapter 5.)

How often do we express words of faith over words

of distress? Bob worked for a company that recently went bankrupt. When asked why the company failed, Bob said it had nothing to do with production problems or poor planning, it had to do with attitude. "It failed because the president displayed so much uncertainty that none of us could work with confidence. He would make a decision and then doubt himself with a lot of "what ifs" followed by hypothetical conflicts. He'd constantly discuss what the competition was doing right, but neglected to share with us how we could learn from that. We were left to soak in his anxiety. I used to joke that our boss needed a personal coach to help him make more positive statements."

The more you practice positive language, the more of a habit it becomes. And one benefit is that you actually *feel* more positive. Whether you're talking out loud, to yourself, or even to your pet, you can lift your spirits just by the attitude with which you speak.

In a *Los Angeles Times* article titled, "Positive Self-Talk Can Be A Super Shot In the Arm," psychologist Rick Blue stresses, "We can talk ourselves into anger, despondency or elation by what we tell ourselves." The key is to really listen to what you are saying, in your head or out loud, and make that language as positive and empowering as possible. People who feel like failures, the article notes, "...often fall into the trap of saying, 'I can't,' 'I'm no good,' 'I'll never win.' And, of course, such expectations fulfill themselves." And the opposite holds true. If you constantly tell yourself, and others, that "I can succeed," "I'm a winner," or "I am capable," then you will rise to those expectations as well.

Certainly, there are other ways to show positiveness. For instance, you can take a potentially negative situation and make it positive, like Jenna's father did with the fireworks. Another way is to make others feel positive by setting an example, choosing to live with passion and spirit.

People crave to be inspired and motivated. Look at the success of Oprah Winfrey. She has become one of the most well-known, powerful, and wealthiest women in the world. And her show is about self-help, problem-solving, and empowerment! Remember the way everyone cheered for Lee Iacocca when he took over Chrysler and saved it? And what about America's obsession with the first Rocky film, a film about the underdog beating all the odds to become a champion. Imagine a world where everybody decided to be positive role models. It starts with attitude. We all have the privilege and choice to look at the bright side of any situation. What choice is yours?

Being An Attractive Person. And now we have come to our final flirting fundamental in our list of nine. Good flirts are attractive. Hmm. Attractive. What does that mean? All flirts have blond hair and blue eyes? All flirts have dark hair and dark eyes? No. All flirts have red hair and green eyes? No, that's not right either. I jest a bit because, truth is, I have no idea what that word "attractive" means. I have taught my flirting course to thousands of people, all of whom I find attractive. And my participants have come in all shapes, sizes, and colors. So, the definition is up to you.

As I tell my audiences, "Be attractive . . . whatever that means to you." If being attractive means wearing all black and a top hat, then that's your definition. If attractive means a conservative suit, there's your definition. If you saw me on a leisurely Sunday you would know that that day, attractive to me is a ripped sweatshirt and shorts, unwashed hair, and no make-up. I glow on those days because I feel happy and relaxed. So, your definition of attractive can vary day to day. The point is: When you feel good, you look good, and the inner peace that you feel inside radiates out.

I have an exercise in my courses where participants write three physical features they really like about themselves. It can be anything: their eyes, waist, wrists, elbows, fingers, toes, nose, chin, feet, knees, hair, earlobes . . . anything! Then I ask if anyone would like to share one of the items on their list. At one workshop for a prestigious financial firm, a gentleman agreed to share one of his features. He stood up slowly with his shoulders back and his head held high. He was wearing a very conservative, designer suit and his hair was groomed to perfection. I asked him to tell us his favorite feature. To our surprise, he said proudly, "My derriere." There was a gasp in the room, then some giggles. "See?" he said, and then he lifted his suit jacket, turned around, and modeled his favorite part for all of us. He was proud, and I could see why. He had a very nice derriere. Everyone agreed, and we gave him a round of applause. Now, because he wore a suit coat most of the time, none of us ever really got to see his derriere, but that didn't matter. He knew it was appealing, and he carried himself with an air of confidence, making an outer glow apparent to us.

Take a minute and list three physical features you really like about yourself, and celebrate them. Isn't that what we do when we're in love? We celebrate! If our partners gain some weight, we say there's just more of them to love. If they get a pimple, we think it's the cutest thing in the world. But when these things happen to us, we treat ourselves with disgust. We need to celebrate ourselves as readily as we are ready to celebrate someone else. That's what beauty is all about.

When we believe we are attractive, we are! Bette Midler, Johnny Carson, Barbra Streisand, and Robin Williams are incredibly attractive people. They draw us to them with their confidence, humor, self-acceptance, and inner strength. So, attractive is not about being a cover model, it's about personal appreciation.

Write down your three favorite features with pride.

1. _____

2. _____

3. _____

_____

3

LIKING
YOURSELF

*"You like me!
You really like me!"*

Sally Field, the actress, shouted this many years ago when she was voted best actress at the Oscars. Aren't we all like that? We all want to feel liked by others, and we want to feel good about ourselves. In the world of flirting, confidence is crucial because we show others how to treat us by the way we treat and value ourselves. If we feel good about who we are, others tend to feel the same way about us. And when we don't feel good about ourselves, it's easy for people to feel the same negative thoughts.

Self-esteem does not come naturally. It needs to be learned and practiced. But when we truly believe in ourselves, we are capable of anything. As David

Schwartz, Ph.D., writes in *The Magic Of Thinking Big*, "Belief is the one basic, absolutely essential ingredient in successful people. Believe, really believe, you can succeed and you will." In the following sections, we will examine how to create personal belief and shape your environments to keep your confidence high.

Try this exercise. Below are two columns. In the left column, write down three words that you feel accurately describe the impression you think you make on others. In other words, if you were to go to a business or social function where you didn't know many people, then mingled for awhile and left, what do you think they would say or think about you? What words would describe you? Outgoing, withdrawn, skeptical, intelligent, energetic, thoughtful? Use any description. Under the right column, write down three words to describe the impression that you'd love to make. If you could make that ideal impression, what it would be? Dynamic? Good listener? Kind? Witty? Be honest.

People See Me As: I'd Like People To See Me As:
1. _____   1. _____
2. _____   2. _____
3. _____   3. _____

Now compare your two lists. Are they fairly similar? Identical? I have done this exercise for hundreds of groups. And in all that time, very few people have had identical lists. That means most people would like to come across differently than they feel they do, and that only a small minority are happy with their first impressions.

The irony in this is that there is only one person who can determine the impression we make on others, and we all know who that is — ourselves. So, if you want to make a certain impression, you must show it, be it, live it. If I want to come across as intelligent, dynamic, and kind, I must behave this way. And the first step to doing this is coaching myself in my mind. "I am intelligent, dynamic, and kind!" The more you repeat a script in your head, the more you'll act it, and the more you'll feel it and become it. We all need to psyche ourselves up, not down.

For the most part, we cannot control our circumstances or other people, but we can control our attitude. And it is attitude, above all else, that determines your level of success. Look at any success story and you'll see it's true. Sally Jessy Raphael, who now has one of the top-rated talk shows, was fired 17 times before she attained her current success. Even Abraham Lincoln failed in eight elections before he won. But, these people made it because they chose the attitude of a champion. So, how do you begin to shape your outlook? Let's begin by taking a closer look at attitudes.

Attitudes are nothing more than habits of thoughts. And habits, just like smoking, exercising, or falling asleep to the TV, can be acquired. Pay attention to the statements you make about yourself in your mind. For instance, as you talk to yourself throughout the day, do you think in a way that is self-promoting or self-defeating?

There was a time in my life where my dominating thoughts were self-defeating. In college I was placed in an honors program for English majors that both flattered and terrified me. I was glad that I had qualified for the program, but I psyched myself out of my own success with such thoughts as, "I'm not as smart as the other students," or "Maybe I can get away with the written assignments, but I'm going to be in big trouble if we have to speak up in class." I allowed myself to focus on every reason why I should have a poor performance. By the time I went to my first class in this program, I was panicked. I sat in the back of the room and never said a word. And every time someone spoke up, I would tell myself, "Compared to what they said, I would have sounded like an idiot."

Looking back, I realize how I had become my own worst enemy. And the irony is, I had no idea I was even doing it. So many of us practice this type of "negative self-talk" constantly without ever taking an objective look at what we're doing to ourselves. What type of dialogue goes through your head? Do you practice positive self-talk or negative?

There was also a time where I practiced positive self-talk and it opened my life to wonderful and new possibilities. In fact, it led to a lifetime of positive self-talk.

Several years ago, a friend and I were set to go to Israel together for 10 days. I was so excited because I had never been there before. Plus, I really needed to get away; I was feeling trapped and unfulfilled in my job and needed some "thinking time" to make some decisions. A week before we were scheduled to leave my friend had to back out, and I was left with a choice that I believe changed my life. To go or not to go. My first instinct was to cancel my ticket because I didn't even think of trying to travel to a foreign country alone. And yet, I was so miserable. I had been looking forward to this trip for such a long time. So, I turned to Plan B: ask someone else to go along. But on such short notice, no one could go. However, a simple comment from one friend who believed in me was the springboard to my newfound confidence. In her brilliant logic she said, "Why don't you go by yourself? You can do it."

I was shocked and inspired. As I said, going alone hadn't even occurred to me until someone said, "You can do it." I kept repeating those words in my head until the "You" became an "I." "I can do it! I can do it! I can do it!" Pretty soon I felt like a reincarnation of "The Little Engine That Could." But, it worked! Moreover, that one small statement of personal belief sprouted more statements of the same kind. "I can do it!" became "I can handle myself with people so I'll be O.K." "I can learn to get around a small city, even a foreign one." "I can travel alone and make friends anywhere." And so on and so on. In my honors course, my personal dialogue had become my own worst enemy, but this time, my personal dialogue was that of someone on my team. I had become my biggest fan. And it all began with one positive statement — one attitude.

The trip was incredible. Sure, I was a bit nervous on the plane and in customs, but I just kept repeating those positive statements. By the end of the trip, I had made some special friends. I had climbed a mountain in blazing heat, and I even began to pick up the language to prepare for a future visit. When I came home, I quit my unfulfilling job, started my own company, which had always been my dream, and found that my personal dialogue had a consistently self-promoting message. My new outlook on life started with one statement of personal belief, which led me to take that trip. From then on, I knew I could do anything. We can always find reasons why we can't. The trick is to find and repeat the reasons why we can and then believe them, and start with small steps.

Fifteen-year-old David Lantz has the right attitude to succeed, according to the *Wall Street Journal*, which profiled him. Why would a national paper for business professionals feature a story on such a young person? Because David has proven himself to be a leading authority in the automobile industry. When he was 11, David tried to convince everyone, from his skeptical classmates to the head of Chrysler, that his newsletter, photocopied and stapled, was an important source of knowledge for this country's automobile industry. He wrote letters to auto publicists, he approached them with business cards, and he always carried subscriptions to his newsletter. And his confidence was evident in his articles, which had the same courage and determination as his marketing efforts. He is known for being honest: "Does Toyota build a car that is not 99% plastic?" he once wrote.

Still, it took time for David's reputation to build. Even classmates thought he was strange when he passed out business cards at lunchtime. But, people began to take notice of his critiques. He was profiled in Chrysler's corporate newsletter and also in a Houston paper. David caught people's attention when he put a photo in his newsletter of himself shaking hands with one of Michigan's biggest automobile moguls, who flew David to his plant for free. He is now praised by leading auto journalists for his outstanding ability in understanding the industry. And David is even expanding his business. He now pays a 14-year-old $20 for each truck review he writes.

David's attitude is his key to success. He is committed, confident, and determined. If a 15-year-old can dare to pursue his dream despite the obstacles around him, why can't we? Starting now, pick and practice an attitude that will keep you trying and believing.

That's exactly what everyone needs to do on a daily basis — adopt an attitude that works. It may not be easy. It takes discipline. But you can do it. You begin to train yourself to think this way by rediscovering your strengths if you've lost sight of them.

Start thinking about the qualities that you really like about yourself or that make you special. Keep in mind these qualities can be anything: you're organized, you have a good laugh, you're a whiz at computers, you're an excellent parent, you're good at details, you're a wonderful friend, you have an excellent phone voice, etc. And also keep in mind that your qualities are also skills, areas that make you unique.

In my case, I've always been teased for my verbal appetite. "Do you ever get tired of talking?" people would ask me. And, I have to admit, I can see their point. I love to talk. But, it was only in recent years that I made the connection that doing something I love could be something I do for a living. And today, I get paid to talk!

People don't realize that looking people in the eye is a skill. Being an organized person is a skill. The ability to think "on your feet" is a skill. Knowing how to listen is a skill. Don't let yourself take your qualities for granted. Start celebrating your attributes by filling in these blanks.

MY STRENGTHS ARE:

1. _____
2. _____
3. _____
4. _____
5. _____

Some people have trouble coming up with five strengths and others get 20 on their first try. If you couldn't come up with five (and I've seen this happen quite often), call a close friend and have him or her help you complete your list. You'd be amazed at the attributes you have which people value but neither you nor they have acknowledged out loud. I once had partners in a law firm tell each other what they valued. One woman was told her constant enthusiasm was much appreciated. She was shocked. "I didn't think anyone cared or noticed!" It's amazing how we keep "warm fuzzies" in.

Now, once you have completed your list, use it as a reminder of your "positives" and as a guideline or boost during the times you feel low or want to "beat yourself up." I taught this exercise to an associate, Susan Broyles, and she has beautifully used it to her advantage. Her five attributes are: she's passionate about things, she's a great friend, she's organized, she's committed to personal growth, and she's funny. One day I was on the phone with Susan and she was having a horrible day. She spent a long time telling me how everything went wrong at work. And she was quite detailed and angry about it. After she vented her frustrations, I tried to cheer her up by suggesting how to get her mind off her troubles. "Why don't you take a walk?" I said. "No! The weather stinks!" she responded. "Our favorite TV show is on soon, why don't you watch it and relax?" my next attempt. "No! I hate that show. It has gotten to be so stupid." Last try. "Go to that restaurant we love, Susan, and treat yourself to a good meal." "Ew! Last time I went there I felt sick." Well, I began to feel frustrated because she seemed stuck in this disconcerting mood. "Sue," I confessed, "I feel badly because I don't know how to help you deal with your anger." Brilliantly focusing on the first strength on her list, she loudly declared, "Jill! I'm not angry. I'm just very passionate!"

It is all what you focus on. I negatively saw Susan's mood as anger, while she chose to see her state of mind as passionate, keeping her self-confidence high. We could all take a lesson from her.

Now that we have learned to focus on our strengths, or at least begun to recognize them, we need a second list — sort of the opposite of our strengths. Some people use the label "problems." Others may call this list shortcomings or weaknesses. However, none of these labels work for enhancement because they keep us stuck. You see, as soon as we label something a problem or a weakness, it seems permanent. The good news is that no one has weaknesses. That's right. Not me, you, nor anybody you know has problems or weaknesses. Now, don't put this book down! I know it sounds idealistic, but I'll explain.

The healthy way to view this exercise is to find a new label for these seemingly pessimistic terms. Here is the answer: *areas that you can improve on*. Again, the word weakness seems more permanent or hopeless. By changing the term to an *area that you can improve on*, you're changing your outlook. Now you can feel positive, strive for growth, and take responsibility to change. An item on my list, for example, is related to one of my strengths; I am an enthusiastic speaker, but in that enthusiasm, I often find myself talking very rapidly. I don't label my "fast-talking" as a problem. Instead, it is an area that I am improving on. That type of thinking helps me slow down.

Now that you have written your list of five (or more) strengths, you can make your second list on areas that you can improve on. In this list, however, write down only three qualities:

AREAS THAT I AM IMPROVING ON:

1. _____
2. _____
3. _____

The point in this exercise is to always keep your strength column longer than the improvement list for two reasons; one is to keep your focus as uplifting and positive as possible to keep your motivation high, and the second reason is so you don't feel overwhelmed with so much self-improvement. You can even have one area that you are working on until it becomes a strength and then concentrate on a new area, etc. All of us have areas of personal growth to work on, and we will our whole lives. The key is keeping your growth in perspective so you focus on your strong attributes. This keeps you feeling confident in yourself and your ability to tackle your less stronger areas.

I am inspired time and time again by the people I meet who have used this method to turn their lives around. I had a meeting with Billy Weisman who owns Weisman Enterprises, a thriving management company in Minneapolis. He was professional, articulate, strong, caring, and intelligent. When I asked what his secret to success was, he said his greatest asset was his dyslexia. I sure didn't expect that. Most people view dyslexia as an obstacle. But, Mr. Weisman chose to turn it into a positive. Because he was unable to read like other people, he found other ways to solve situations. "My dyslexia helped me become an effective problem solver." And he built his million dollar company with that skill.

Michael Jordan admits he was glad that he was cut from his high school basketball team. Being cut, he says, made him work harder and redefine his goals to help him become an outstanding player. *Success* magazine in July 1990 praised Lois Benjamin-Bohm who, in the face of tragedy, turned a small company into a $2 million business. Over 11 years, she and her husband had built a moving and storage company. Then, suddenly, he and their three children were killed in a car accident. Lois was devastated and numbed with grief. Still, she forced herself to pick up the pieces and take over the small company. She wanted to quit so many times, but never did. She had come to a decision. "You have to make a choice somewhere to go forward. If you don't make that choice, you become a victim."

At this time, you may be going through a difficult period: a job move, ending a relationship, a health problem, whatever. Perhaps you're experiencing problems on a smaller scale: you may not be allocating your time properly, you feel overweight, a valued co-worker just quit the company. Regardless of the challenge, we are constantly dealing with difficult issues, which often bring unexpected abrupt change or personal confusion, factors that can affect our esteem.

One way we can try to maintain a healthy sense of confidence through difficult periods is by shaping our attitudes. We can ask ourselves, "What am I learning from this?" or "How has this experience helped me grow?" Turn "This is awful! I'm going crazy" into "This is scary but I will survive this as a stronger and wiser person." What you need to remember about a crisis is that you grow most when facing one. However, most people allow themselves to feel overwhelmed by crisis or personal mistakes.

In a Baltimore Sun article titled "To Err is (Very) Human So Lighten Up," author and self-made millionaire Richard Brodie comments, "I think people are programmed to magnify failure beyond all proportions. But to be a success in life you need to encounter failure more than people who are just content to survive. In fact, when a failure occurs, you can pat yourself on the back and say, 'Wow, I'm taking risks towards what I want in life.'"

While such advice is helpful and true, it certainly is difficult to remember that you are growing during a crisis because it's often a time of heightened emotions, even depression. That's where a written exercise can help because writing thoughts down, in addition to helping you clear your thoughts, also helps you take an objective view. One article on the importance of journal writing went so far as to say, "Writing our thoughts down can be just as effective and healthy as therapy with a licensed professional can be." Here is one way to look at a crisis in a positive sense through writing. Fill in the blank after each sentence:

I am learning from this dilemma that

_____

OR
The ways this crisis is making me stronger are

_____

I also use a similar written exercise in my seminars to examine our past issues and how they have positively impacted us:

The worst crisis I have ever been through is

_____

AND
What I learned from it was

_____

It's inspiring to realize how much a job loss or accident can turn your life around positively in the long run. After this exercise, one seminar participant approached me and said, "Years ago my mother had an aneurysm. It devastated my whole family. We didn't even know if she was going to make it. At the time, I didn't think about what I was learning, but after writing it down, I realized what a better son I've become since the crisis and how I treat my mother better and appreciate her so much more than I had before all that happened."

During one particular self-esteem seminar for teenagers, I had them do the previous exercise verbally. They separated into pairs and told their partners about a crisis in their life and what they learned from it. I had no idea this would be such a moving experience for these young people — most of the participants were crying when they shared their problems. When I asked what they learned from the exercise, I was surprised by their comments. It wasn't so much the realization that problems could help them grow; instead, the real lesson was that they learned how good it feels to talk about pain and share it. "You realize you're not the only one who has a tough time with your mom and dad," as one young man so eloquently said.

So, here is a valuable lesson in keeping your confidence high: Have at least one person in your life with whom you can share your problems openly and honestly. And make sure that person is supportive, and a healthy individual to turn to. The whole concept of support groups is based on the notion that we can solve our problems easier, and nurture our self-esteem, in an environment of openness, empathy, sharing, and commitment to personal growth.

It's important to surround yourself with people who believe in you. Take your emotional temperature around the people in your life who affect you greatly, be it your boss, mate, or best friend, and ask yourself how you feel around this person. Are your personal relationships in your best interest?

For my self-esteem seminars, I have participants make a list of the five most influential relationships in their life. For example, a list could look like this:

1. Mom
2. John (husband)
3. Sue (boss)
4. Steve (brother)
5. Tim (best friend)

Then I have them complete this next sentence:

When I'm around [fill in name of person from previous list] I feel _____

_____

_____.

(fill in the second blank with the true emotions you generally feel around this person be it nervous, threatened, accepted, loved, encouraged, skeptical, etc.)

Now, it's your turn.

THE FIVE MOST INFLUENTIAL RELATIONSHIPS
IN MY LIFE ARE:
1.
2.
3.
4.
5.
When I'm around _____, I feel _____
_____.

The key is to be honest, even if you don't like what you're discovering. Perhaps you feel nervous around your mate or threatened by your best friends. Many people remove themselves so far from their deepest gut feelings or inner voice that they don't even realize how badly they feel around the people who supposedly are the best for them. This emotional separation makes sense. Who wants to face the fact that their parents make them feel uncomfortable or their mate is unsupportive? In order to cope with these painful gut feelings, people often distance themselves so far from their emotions that they stay in an unhealthy cycle without knowing it.

This exercise is not meant to destroy your close relationships, but to make you aware of your feelings and to take action to make those relationships healthy and supportive. For some of us, this exercise will make us communicate more with the people around us, to create a stronger bond of mutual self-esteem. Others may find they need to form new friendships entirely if an effort of honest communication does not enhance the relationship.

Someone once said, "YOUR RELATIONSHIPS ARE AS HEALTHY AS YOU ARE." Everyone deserves to be valued, appreciated, and accepted unconditionally. I hope your personal relationships do that for you.

In addition to personal relationships, another area in people's lives where they frequently struggle to keep their self-esteem high is in their jobs. Some people work in environments where there is a great lack of recognition or appreciation. For some, a compliment from their boss is when she says nothing. When the boss does speak, it's usually to point out an error. Sound familiar?

So how do you stay motivated at a less-than-satisfying job? The answer is to look within yourself and ask yourself: what can I do to motivate me? How can I bring purpose to my work? There are many ways to re-motivate yourself on a daily basis. Richard Kelly is a model example of an individual finding achievement and meaning in his work regardless of title or salary. Richard worked at the Jewel supermarket outside of Chicago for 35 years and never moved higher than grocery sacker in the company ladder. Here's an article on the man for your inspiration.

One American's way: Work, be helpful.

Success has more than one definition. Just ask a man who is about to retire from bagging groceries.

By Bob Secter
TIMES STAFF WRITER

NORTHBROOK, Ill. — Corporate America — smarmy, leveraged, cutthroat America; discount, high-volume, bargain-price, service-with-a-snarl America — could sure learn a thing or two from Richard Kelly.

For starters, he is living proof that status and a fast buck need not be the only barometers of success in today's marketplace. Kelly, pushing 60, has spent more than 35 years at the Jewel supermarket in this well-heeled Chicago suburb and has never moved higher than grocery sacker on the organizational ladder.

Still, with a smile and a hustle and an out-of-fashion notion that work, courtesy and loyalty are their own rewards, he has managed to become probably the most revered grocery sacker around.

A competitor once tried in vain to steal him away from Jewel with promises of shorter hours and higher pay. Pat Nufer, a customer, pointed to Kelly as a role model for her children while they were growing up.

Now, with Kelly planning to retire this month, store manager Trey Johnson is, frankly, worried that business might drop off without his modest but popular bagger, a man who brings a refreshing breath of personal charm to an increasingly sterile, bar-code-scanner world.

Kelly knows whole generations of shoppers by name, hands lollipops to the children and is always there to retrieve the glove that someone dropped or hold the squirming baby while Mom fishes in her purse for the car keys.

Johnson, who was not yet born when Kelly bagged his first pot roast here, recalled the way one longtime customer summed up Kelly the other day: "I can't figure out what it is about Kelly. I can't put my finger on it . . . but he's a great man."

Kelly's secrets to success? For one, don't be satisfied with just putting the bread and eggs on top. Make sure everything in the bag is square and tight. That way, it's less likely to tip and spill all over the car trunk on the way home.

As much as Kelly knows parcels, he knows people even better. In the kind of job where longevity is measured in months, not decades, and a veteran is anyone who can legally buy a beer, Kelly has grown old with his customers. He's gotten to know their children and grandchildren, as well as their troubles and triumphs.

He doesn't just lug their purchases out to the parking lot. He has watched their houses when they were on vacation, cleaned their gutters and mopped their basements when the sewers backed up, and even driven the sick to the hospital.

"The average person looks down on a job like this," Kelly said, "but whatever your hand finds to do, do with all thy might. That's in Ecclesiastes. I may not do it as good as other people, but I'm doing the best I can."

Humble, for sure, but nobody's fool. Back in 1956, Kelly was a night shift orderly at a Veteran's Administration hospital. His wife became pregnant with the first of their three children and he needed to make extra money to pay for the delivery. So he went to see the company commander of his army reserve unit, who, in civilian life, managed the

Northbrook Jewel market. He had been after Kelly for months to come to work for him as a stock boy in the store.

At first, Kelly planned to work only long enough to cover the hospital bill, but then he got the idea that if he kept both jobs he might be able to scrape together enough money to buy a house. By 1958, he had that home, but still he didn't quit.

Over the years, he has acquired seven houses, which he rents out. He started a landscaping business, and continued to work days at Jewel and nights at the hospital until last year, when he retired from the hospital. He also cleaned gutters and did other odd jobs, often for people who had come to know him through the grocery.

Scampering around the checkout counters all these years has helped Kelly form a refreshingly simple but winning philosophy about what it takes to get ahead, one that might be worth a passel of high-priced consultants reports. Some of his thoughts:

"It's the small things that count. The big things take care of themselves. If a lady drops her keys, you try to be the person to pick them up. If my wife came in to shop, I would like it if somebody put everything in the car for her, and did it without any attitude.

"Too many people today, it seems like they want to get paid but they don't want to work. They want a position but they don't want to work for it. But if I don't get nowhere I can't blame you. I blame me. I'm my biggest supporter. I'm my biggest hindrance."

Now, preparing to hang up his smock this week, Kelly said: "There's other things to do. A lot of old people need some help. Maybe I can go out and talk to some boys on the street and turn their lives around."

Kelly's customers — his friends, really — say they understand, but they are sad to see him go, nevertheless. "Kelly's special," said Debbie Anderson. "He's been here since my children were born. I have a 12-year-old and a 9-year-old, and they still look forward to coming here and getting their sucker after all these years."

"If Kelly's leaving, we'll leave, too," another customer joked. "We've known him for 26 years . . . putting the groceries and the kids in and out of the car for me. One day, one of my kids said something about him having an inferior job and I said, 'Wait a minute! He does something important.' He's one of the nicest people you'll ever want to meet. He'll never be replaced. They can fill his hours, but not his shoes."

Clearly, Richard Kelly is a man who took a position, what some may consider "common," and made it the most important job in the company. He is a classic example that true self-worth and professionalism have nothing to do with job title.

Another person who has done just that is Leslie, a receptionist for Tom Peters, a well-known author and speaker on excellence. In one memorable article, Tom wrote about her:

"I've never seen her resume. Leslie may well have a Ph.D. in nuclear physics from Cal Tech. Or she may have not made it through the fourth grade. But she has taken our company and turned it around. That's right, our receptionist is a genuine turnaround artist."

Peters goes on to sing the praises of Leslie, commenting on her style: upbeat, courteous, funny, patient, upstanding, professional, smart, outrageous, etc. He goes on about how she does the extra things like doing additional research for a client just to be helpful. Or always making sure a call goes to the right person.

> " . . . what an enormous difference one person can make in the spirit of an organization. Energy and enthusiasm really are 'everything' and have little to do with job title."

Both Leslie and Richard Kelly are excellent examples of how motivation comes from within, and how flirting — creating a warm, honest, and sincere rapport to build your self-esteem and the self-esteem in others — is so important to success.

So how do you motivate yourself? In the next several pages, we will examine 11 different ways to remotivate ourselves. And instead of focusing on the Lee Iacoccas or the Michael Jordans of this world, we'll hear true stories from people just like us who found new reasons to like themselves during difficult times.

1. ***Knowledge***: We often take learning for granted, but it's amazing to see how a new piece of information can make us feel re-motivated about our jobs all over again.

   Amy Spielman, of Vector Marketing, told me how knowledge saved her sales career. She explained, "When I first started as a sales rep, I dreaded the 'close' because I always felt I lost the customer's interest at that point. I became so fearful of 'closing', in fact, that I just skipped it after spending so much time trying to make an effective presentation. Of course, I never sold any merchandise without asking for the sale. And because I wasn't making any sales, I stopped calling on people and I came close to quitting altogether. My problem was simple — lack of knowledge. Luckily, my manager called me in to discuss my results. 'How come I don't see any sales from you?' he asked. 'I guess I just can't do this.' I was so discouraged. I felt completely unmotivated to solve my problem. My manager was persistent. 'Where do you think the problem lies?' 'Well, they seem excited during the presentation, but when I get to the end they seem to lose interest.' 'Hmm,' my manager began, 'let's see your closing.' As I went through my close reluctantly, I noticed my manager grinning. 'See. You're laughing at me because I can't do this,' I complained. 'No,' he responded, 'I'm grinning because I see where you're going wrong.' He went on to explain that I memorized the close so well that it sounded fake and rehearsed. He helped me re-learn it so that it sounded natural. I began to slow down as I spoke, and I added pauses where I had none before. He also helped me understand each part of the close and why I was saying it. After our meeting, I was unstoppable. That afternoon, I went on five sales calls. I sold on four. Best of all, I couldn't wait to get to the close."

An acquaintance of mine has been with the same financial firm for 20 years. Marveling at his endurance I once asked him, "Have you ever felt like you were in a rut?" "There is too much to learn to get caught in a rut," he told me. He said he attended as many seminars on his industry that he could. He also spoke highly of a number of sales tapes and books on related subjects. "Every time I learn a new sales pitch or read about a successful negotiation, I get hungry to try some new tactics myself," he boasted. It's true. Knowledge inspires. Perhaps we can all re-inspire ourselves through knowledge. One way is through continuing education.

There are usually an array of classes, audio tapes, and video tapes on subjects related to many particular occupations. Best of all, seminars, books, and tapes are accessible to everybody. And though your company may not provide such materials, you can find books and tapes at any library, or locate inexpensive courses through various continuing education facilities.

I'll never forget how gratifying it felt to hear the comments of one of my flirting course participants. She must have been in her late 50's and had taken the course to enhance her social skills. While most of the other students were younger and eager to learn more about business skills, this woman didn't seem to mind; she was able to take the information and mold it to her social life. On the way out she squeezed my arm excitedly and whispered, "I can't wait to take this information and try it out!" Education had motivated her. Learn about whatever excites you. If re-educating yourself about your career doesn't excite you, educate yourself on something that does. Every new piece of knowledge can affect the "big picture." Knowledge empowers us.

2. **Recognition**: A little recognition goes a long way. Marshall Peterson, a counselor who works with children, explains, "I once taught a four-part course for young adults on self-esteem. Most of the course's format was in discussion form. There were 14 students in the class and all but one gave input during the first two sessions. The one student who never spoke up always sat in the back of the room and took the role of an apathetic observer. After the second session, I asked this particular student on his way out how he felt about the class. 'It's O.K.' he responded. 'You know, John,' I added, 'I'd love to hear your input sometimes.' 'I haven't had anything to say,' John remarked. However, I believed John really meant that he didn't think he had anything valuable to add. Perhaps all he needed was a little encouragement.

"When we met for the third session, to John's surprise I called on him. We were having a discussion about why some people bully or feel they need to be critical of other people. 'Who knows why some people do this?' "Cuz they want attention?' one student chimed in. 'Definitely,' I added. 'What other reason could there be? John, how about you? Any ideas?' At first John shrugged his shoulders in silence. Not wanting to push him, I looked around the room inviting other students to comment when suddenly I heard John begin to speak quietly. 'People who pick on other people think it makes them look better. If they cut somebody else down, then they think they look good.' 'Excellent answer,' I exclaimed. 'Did everyone hear that?' My enthusiastic validation brought changes in John. He began to sit up straighter and look at the other students. As I rephrased what John said and explained it's accuracy, I noticed John begin to smile. For the remainder of that session, I was delighted to see John raise his hand three times. Each time he was called on, he had added very thoughtful input and I made sure I let him know that. When the students were leaving class this time, I told John he did a wonderful job. He blushed and said thanks. This was not the same indifferent student from the first session. John had become willing, enthusiastic, and alert. All he needed was a little recognition. And the more worthwhile he felt, the more motivated he was to try even harder."

Many of us are like John. At one time or another we have all come to a place in our jobs where we felt like our opinions didn't matter. And the more we felt that we were not making any impact, the less motivated we felt to try. Time and time I hear stories of frustrated employees who feel that they never get any credit for their efforts. The less appreciated they feel, the less motivated they are. Just imagine how much productivity would increase for companies who would switch over to managing on positive reinforcement rather than negative. Take a close look, in fact, at most sales organizations and watch how heavily they rely on recognition as a motivator.

I remember one of the main factors that motivated me at my first sales job. If I did a good job, I would be recognized in front of my peers at the next sales meeting. If there was a contest, it was exciting to put my "best foot forward" because I could win a great trophy or see my name in the company newsletter. This type of validation meant more to me than even a raise could because it made me feel that I was worthwhile and appreciated. So, when I became a manager I employed the same techniques. We created an office newsletter and special contests to reward reps for their efforts. I saw one sales rep work harder than he claimed "he ever had" all because he wanted to see his name at the top of the newsletter.

Aside from the fact that these types of promotions increased our office productivity, one bonus for me was that recognition is free! It cost me nothing to acknowledge someone with applause at a sales meeting, or just mention out loud what a good job so-and-so made on her sales calls last week. Even a newsletter is inexpensive. I am convinced that the morale of our country would be higher if all companies started valuing their employees just a little more. Since so much of our self-esteem in this culture seems to be based on "what we do," then "what we do" needs to enhance our self-esteem, not destroy it.

This brings me to the notion of personal responsibility. How can you create recognition for yourself if you work in an environment where there seems to be none? There are many ways to tackle this. First, you can go to the people in charge and propose some type of contest or newsletter, explaining that such programs would enhance the company productivity as well. If you feel your boss is not approachable, get a group of people together in your firm and create contests, a newsletter, or some type of forum that deals with recognition. You can also set personal goals for yourself at work and share those goals with your family or loved ones. We all deserve to be valued and appreciated for our efforts. If you are working in an environment that does not embrace this notion, take action to get some recognition. A little attention goes a long way!

3. **Challenge**: One good thing about the "work environment" is that in order for most companies to grow and profit, they need to respond to the changes of the world by adding new technology or implementing new programs. So, hopefully, you have had to take on new challenges at work to keep up with your particular industry. Some people's jobs have thrown them into a "rut" because they have done the same thing for so long. If that's your case, take it upon yourself to bring challenges to your work. Perhaps you can find a way to expand your job description in order to add new elements of creativity to your work.

Terry Russo had been in the same job for eight years and was beginning to feel unmotivated since he had mastered most of the elements of his work. He talked to his supervisors and they decided to give him a responsibility that had been run by another department. This new responsibility dealt with advertising, an area he had never been a part of before. He quickly became fascinated about the ins and outs of advertising. What works, what doesn't, how people interpret ads, why placement of ads is so important. Terry's new responsibilities made him feel like a kid in school. "I'm just fascinated," he said. "It feels like I have a whole new dimension to what I do." Indeed, challenge adds dimension. Terry was fortunate to have supervisors who listened to him.

In addition to finding challenges at work, you can enhance your feelings of worth and stimulation by finding challenges outside of work. Taking classes, joining a sports team or book-of-the-month club, finding a hobby are all ways to add new dimensions to your life. For many, challenges outside of work enhance our job performance. Whether we find our challenges at work or in our hobbies, everyone needs a sense of new stimulation when things become routine. What challenges can you create?

4. *Power:* The notion of power has taken a "bum rap" in the past. Indeed, power can be dangerous when used as negative manipulation or abuse. On the other hand, power can be wonderful when it is channeled into a positive direction. And while some people may have been raised to feel that "power corrupts," when you take a closer look, you realize that everyone craves a sense of feeling powerful. Feeling powerful, in a healthy sense, is feeling self-assured, worthwhile, and valuable.

When a marvelous secretary I had for two years told me she was considering finding another job, I felt great concern as I didn't want to lose her. I asked her what I could do to help her want to stay. "We really need you, Heidi," I began. "You are so valuable to our office," and I went on to list the reasons why. When I was through, I concluded that I couldn't imagine working without her. She seemed delighted but shocked.

"Wow. I didn't know I was so important. You've just made me feel so special, so powerful." During our talk, not only did we solve the problem of Heidi's disillusionment, but she felt so "powerful" that she took it upon herself to be instrumental in our problem solving.

After a candid discussion, I learned that Heidi was feeling overworked. She claimed that she had to spend so much time answering the phones that she was unable to do her paperwork. We agreed that we needed another person to help with the phones. "I'd like to write the advertisement for the new person and do the interviews with you," Heidi suggested, "since I'll be working with the new person closely." Heidi used her new-found feeling of power in extremely positive ways: to keep her confidence high and to make my role in the hiring process a lot easier.

Darla Zais shared her newfound views on power with me. She explained, "Before I learned how to use a computer, I typed most of my materials and then hired a woman, Lisa Fuller, who has a word processing business, to put it on a computer for me. Finally, I decided it was about time I get over my technology fear and invest in a computer myself. Since Lisa had given me such great service, I asked her if she would give me an hour lesson on the computer. She agreed. When I asked her how much she would charge she said, 'Nothing. I like teaching people. Don't worry about it.'

"Despite her reassurance, I felt guilty about this free lesson, especially because I was beyond being computer illiterate. I was computer ignorant, and it showed. While she was instructing me, I felt dizzy and discouraged. 'Lisa, this is all so complicated!' I whined. 'Darla, you'll get it. One hour isn't enough time to feel completely comfortable. Hang in there.' My guilt grew deeper. Not only was I taking her time, I was a slow learner. When the lesson was over, I was sure I was more confused than when we started, but I was mistaken! The next day I mustered up the courage to try it on my own and lo and behold, I had picked up more than I thought. Yesirree, I was opening files and closing files, I was saving and deleting, I was bolding and underlining — the works! I had to share my excitement with Lisa. I called her up and told her how thrilled I was. She responded, 'Thanks! You make me feel so powerful.'"

Heidi and Lisa are examples of how "empowering others" is one of the best ways to feel a sense of strength. If you're feeling unmotivated at work and need to regain that sense of power, try teaching or sharing with others what you know. Volunteer to train a new employee or reach out to co-workers who are having problems.

5. *Independence*: So many people look at their jobs in terms of "have to's." "I have to be at work by nine." "I have to work late today." "I

have to get this report done on time."
Unfortunately, when we focus so much on the
obligations of our work, we lose sight of the freedom or independence that our work provides us.

After interviewing people in various occupations,
I was surprised and impressed at the ways some
of us have discovered independence in our
work. One outside sales rep commented that he
looks forward to his driving time in between
appointments. "It gives me a chance to collect
my thoughts while I'm by myself. I also like to
play my favorite motivational tapes in the car
and coach myself before the next meeting."

A busy marketing executive confessed to me,
"When things get really crazy around the office,
I'll often take my own 'time-out' by shutting my
door and holding all calls. I like being in charge
and choosing my break time."

A news reporter mentioned to me, "I get a real
sense of freedom by taking a news story and
shaping it in my own style."

So what do you do if your work isn't giving you
the sense of independence you crave? Ask Liz
Reeves, who found another solution. "I work
closely with people all day. Independence to me
means alone time, quiet time. I get that urge
satisfied by my hobby — reading. Sure, it's a
simple hobby, but it provides so much for me. I
read by myself in a quiet room. I read what I

want. How fast or slow I want. And if I decide to skip some pages, that's all up to me. Plus, I can completely escape for awhile, without having to go anywhere. My books give me a tremendous sense of freedom."

How about you? How does your job give you a sense of independence? I've even talked to commuters who have found great independence just by riding the train to work. But if you are like Liz, who finds little independence at work, try her method. Find a hobby or activity that can be an outlet for your independence, whether it's reading, walking, or singing in the shower. Take some time to have some freedom.

6. ***Accomplishment***: I think everyone has, at one time or another, reached the end of the day and found themselves feeling down, thinking these thoughts, "Hmm. I didn't get anything done today." We tend to be hard on ourselves when we feel that we've been unproductive. Conversely, when we've had days or weeks that have been highly productive, we feel extremely good about ourselves. Why is this so?

One reason may be that we live in a culture that places importance on personal progress and goal achievement. A second reason is human nature, which dictates that a large part of feeling worthwhile as an individual depends on our sense of personal achievement. Most of us simply feel better about ourselves when we are "accomplishing." That's why our jobs, careers, or just the notion of "working" is a vital link to our self-esteem and has become a main source of personal motivation.

Jan Hains, a freelance writer, had a six-week project where she practically worked around the clock. During that time she kept telling me, "Jill, I need a vacation so badly. I can't wait to just do nothing." When the project ended, Jan enjoyed her freedom for about a week. Then she began to feel restless, which surprised me because she seemed so busy. She was running around town, seeing friends whom she hadn't seen for a while, seeing movies and shopping.

"I feel so antsy," she told me one day. "Antsy? Gosh, you seem so busy, though. Every time I talk to you, you're dashing off somewhere. How come you feel bored?" "It's not boredom," Jan said. "It's ... well, I just don't feel like I'm doing anything. Maybe I need to feel more productive. But my next project doesn't start for two weeks." "Well," I asked, "could you try being productive at home?" And wouldn't you know it, by the next time I had talked to her, she had cleaned out her closets, painted the garage, rearranged her furniture, and laid new kitchen tile. After reporting this impressive list to me, I asked, "Now do you still feel antsy?" "Not as much as before, but I still miss working."

You can see Jan's point. "Working" does give us a tremendous sense of accomplishment. Jan craved to return to a freelance project because that's what she needed to feel that sense of deep accomplishment she was missing. But Jan's definition of working meant earning a pay check, doing projects that were career-related, getting out of the house. For others, working can mean something else.

Herbert Seder had worked as an investment banker for 30 years. He always enjoyed the challenges of his job, along with the structure it gave his life. But now it was time to retire. What would he do with all that time on his hands? Herbert knew that many of his peers looked forward to retirement, but he wanted to work, he wanted structure, and he longed for a continued sense of accomplishment.

The first week of his retirement, Herbert was already restless. Then an idea struck him. As he was flipping channels on the T.V., he caught a public access talk show. The sets were basic, and the host was certainly no Johnny Carson. But still, it was fascinating. "I could do that," Herbert thought to himself. "Hey, I could do that!" Herbert checked into getting involved in public access T.V., and it was easier than he had anticipated. The station would provide him a production crew and times to use the facility. All he had to do was produce the show. But what would the show be about?

You could have guessed. Indeed, we find our art through our life and Herbert decided to make his show about retirement. He created segments about everything from hobbies to vacations, and he had guests tell their own personal stories, which provided much of the program's humor. He called the show, "So What Do I Do Now?" And he relished every moment from the taping of the show, to researching a topic, to finding the guests. The best part of all? It was so much fun and gave him a sense of accomplishment like he had never felt before. In fact, six months after his retirement, an investment firm contacted him and asked if he would consult for them. The money they offered was quite substantial, but Herbert turned them down. "I'm sorry. I'm too busy working on my show."

Accomplishment is a great feeling and a powerful motivator. When I first started my career as a speaker, things were slow at first. In the meantime, to maintain my esteem and feelings of productivity, I began each day with what I called my "balance list." Each day I tried to accomplish things in five areas of my life. (1) I'll do something for my career, whether it's making a contact or working on a promotional piece; (2) I'll learn something new, whether it's a new word or how to fix my car; (3) I'll do some exercise, whether it's a brief walk or an aerobics class; (4) I'll do something for a friend, whether it's a favor or sending a card; and (5) I'll do something indulgent for myself, whether it's eating a sundae or renting a comedy. The list not only put a sense of balance in my life, it also gave me my sense of productivity.

Now you may be saying to yourself, "I do that stuff every day." Most of us do. But for me, at the time, turning it into a list was the visual reinforcement I needed to feel I was achieving. If you feel that you're not accomplishing a lot at work, try making a list of things you want to get done. Even if you check off only three items, you may find that you are doing more than you thought.

If you feel that no matter what you try, your job just isn't giving you that sense of accomplishment and satisfaction that you crave, take on a hobby. One woman I know felt she didn't have time for an intense hobby so she joined a book-of-the-month club that required her to read one book monthly and meet twice a month to discuss it. She just read a few pages every night and the meetings were only two hours. She felt a great accomplishment by reading and learning. Better still, the productivity in her new hobby took the frustration away when she felt less productive at her job.

We all need to accomplish things to help our esteem and keep our motivation running. Whether it's lists, jobs, or outside interests, tap into what makes you tick and create your own arena of accomplishment.

7. **Relationships**: As we look back on our lives so far it's amazing to comprehend all the families we've been in. (All the families, you may being saying to yourself?) Yes. Certainly we're aware of our immediate families — the families we were born into — and, of course, as we marry, or as brothers and sisters marry, we take on extended families as well. But the people that we often fail to identify as family are the individuals with whom we spend 40 hours a week. Our work family. And just like our immediate families, while we may grow fond of those familiar faces at work, these are also the people who, at times, drive us crazy. Still, these are also the people who we care a great deal about.

If it weren't for our jobs, many of us would never have made some of our most influential relationships. We all have that boss, co-worker, receptionist, or janitor, who we will never forget. Even the stormy and agonizing relationships at work have had a great effect on our character and our personal growth. That's why the workforce is one of the greatest training grounds for learning to deal with and appreciate people.

Marshall Keensen, of New York, could not find the strength to fire Dane. They had worked together over five years and had seen one another go through many successes and failures. To Marshall, firing Dane felt more like he was abandoning him, like tossing aside one's son. The two men met in 1986 when Marshall was promoted to run his own territory for the firm. He needed to hire and develop his own staff and Dane impressed him right from the first interview. Though only 23, Dane had charisma. He could light up a room in seconds and get people excited about things. He had the potential to be a great salesman. And even though he was a little "rough around the edges," he definitely had talent. Marshall hired him. His instincts were right. Dane was a phenomenal salesman. He broke company records repeatedly, and was driven beyond expectations. He wanted to be number one, and hoped to one day have Marshall's position. Dane watched everything Marshall did and listened to everything he said. This, of course, made Marshall that much more fond of him.

After three years, Dane was promoted to branch manager, with Marshall as his immediate supervisor. Both men were excited about the challenge and confident it would be a great move for themselves and the company profits. They were wrong. Just two weeks into the job, Marshall began noticing changes in Dane. His numbers were low and he didn't come to Marshall for help, which he had always done before. Furthermore, Dane never seemed to be in the office. Every time Marshall would call, Dane was out. Marshall was disturbed. He set up a review with Dane to learn what was going on and to help him regain momentum.

Dane was deeply apologetic and insisted it was the stress of a new position. He took careful notes during the review and promised he would get things straight. It didn't happen. Things got worse as two of Dane's employees quit. They sent Marshall a note about Dane's difficult and often offensive behavior. Marshall not only felt frustrated, but hurt. He believed in Dane and gave him a chance. What was happening? Eventually Marshall learned that Dane was using drugs. Marshall was crushed. After too many warnings, Marshall had to let Dane go. He tried to get the company to pay for Dane's treatment, but Dane refused to admit he needed help.

Yes, earlier I talked about how work can lead us into wonderful new families, and I've just told you a story about disappointment and pain. Marshall still says he feels bad when he thinks about what happened, but he claims the experience taught him a great deal. He now maintains a sense of professional distance from his staff, after learning the dangers of getting too personally involved. And, he is much more logical and thorough before promoting someone. He makes sure they are also prepared for the challenge emotionally.

Like family relationships, work relationships are powerful. We find ourselves loving, hating, questioning these people who have become such integral parts of our lives. With every relationship we learn and we grow. A lot of us have found wonderful friends and role models through work. So, enjoy these extended families that our work world brings us. And flirt with your work family. In the long run, we will not remember the paycheck we got in 1989 or the day we left work early, we'll remember the people we saw everyday and what they meant to us.

8. ***Creativity***: When I was 18 I took a job selling shoes in an upscale women's shoe store. One day a young woman and her mother came into the store. The daughter was extremely tall. In her hand she had a white piece of lace. She looked a little stressed. "Can you help me?" she asked me and my manager. "I'm getting married and if I wear anything higher than a flat I'll be taller than the groom." "These are all the flats we have," my manager said, pointing to our selection. "They're not that dressy, but our short heels are so short that you'll never feel any extra height. Here are a few beautiful pairs," she said dashing off to grab some short-heeled shoes. As she walked past me she snapped, "Now watch me closely," hoping I would learn something.

I looked back at the mother and daughter and noticed how upset the daughter looked. She whispered to her mother, "This happens wherever we go. All I want is a pretty flat. I don't want any heel!" "I've got an idea," I said. "Let's take another look at the flat selection and see if we can come up with something."

As we looked over the flat shoes, my manager joined us and shot me a dirty glance. The daughter held up a shoe, "I really like this one, and the color is perfect. It's just a little bland." My manager gave me an "I told you so" expression. As I looked at her, her big, flashy earring caught my attention. ("Sometime I'd like to clip her mouth together with that," I thought.) Suddenly my evil thoughts turned into inspiration. "We'll just have to dress up the shoe!" I looked at the earrings the mother was wearing and they were stylish and appropriate. "Can I borrow your earring?" She handed it to me and I clipped it on the front of the shoe. Suddenly we had the look we wanted. "I love it!" the girl shouted. They bought the shoes and came back into the store an hour later to show me the earrings they bought to match the shoe. We laughed at our new fashion statement and the mother turned to me and said, "You are so creative."

I learned a valuable lesson that day. I used to think of creativity in terms of art. Sculptors, painters, musicians, writers — now they work in fields where you can be creative. But it never dawned on me that creative expression can be showed in many styles and forms regardless of the medium or field.

Once I allowed myself creative expression at the shoe store, not only was the job more interesting, but my confidence grew, my sales increased, and the range of my ideas seemed limitless. From that day on I was designing more "earring shoes" for other customers. I was thinking of new and clever ways to explain the benefits of our footwear and I even snazzed up our store display. I was no longer only a salesperson, I was an artist!

Celeste Wolff, of Chicago, worked many years for a record company. Every year her firm held company meetings where representatives from the various music types (classical, alternative, R&B, rap) would give reports on what was happening in their particular sector. Unfortunately, the reports all seemed to follow the same format and, at one meeting in particular, didn't do much to keep people's attention. By the time the rep for country music had his turn, it was very late in the evening. Knowing that at that point no one cared, he gave his report sarcastically. Ironically, his sarcastic tone made his report a bit more interesting and Celeste noticed people were chuckling and paying more attention than usual. She began to brainstorm.

The second set of reports were scheduled for the next evening and Celeste was to speak number four out of six. Back at her hotel room, she turned on the T.V. to David Letterman's nightly top ten list and something in her head clicked. "I'm going for it," she decided. The next night came and the reports were the same usual thing. As expected, people were growing restless. Then it was Celeste's turn. She walked up to the podium with a tape recorder in hand. She pressed play and all of a sudden the David Letterman Show theme song pumped through the room. Then, the theme song faded into a melodic, slow rap beat that served as the background music for her report. "Here are the top ten reasons to support the exciting trends in the rap music scene," Celeste began. From the outset, the audience was enthralled. This was different. "Number ten," Celeste began. Each comment she made was informative and extremely funny. While she educated, she also entertained and amused. At the end of her report she got the first and only standing ovation. "Thank God, you're original," one colleague said to her on the way out. "I was beginning to fall asleep." "Very ingenious," someone else commented. "I'm never going to give a lame report again after what you did tonight."

All Celeste did was take a conventional format and give it a creative twist, and yet she not only impacted her own motivation and confidence, she inspired many others. In fact, after the next year's meeting, she told me, "Jill, it was a riot. It was like a contest. Each person topped the next. One guy gave his report in a newscast-type skit, and the country rep gave his report in country slang. Everyone loved it. It was the best conference we've had."

Freedom is exactly what happened to a group of corporate executives when they were introduced to a new way of dealing with workplace stress — singing. At a conference titled, *"How to be Creative in the Workplace,"* executives from Fortune 500 companies gathered to learn creative strategies to use in the workplace. They knew they were going to listen to various speakers that day, but they had no idea singing would be involved.

When the mid-morning speaker approached the podium, she was not holding the old usual stack of notes, but instead, a guitar. The audience whispered in nervous anticipation as she introduced herself and asked them to pull out their song sheets. The speaker started to sing and play her guitar.

It took a few minutes, but soon 150 executives were singing along, loudly and proudly. She encouraged them to hold hands. And, in moments, they were swaying in unison. The president of one of the top chemical dependency institutions was holding the hand of a beer company C.E.O. And competing insurance salespeople were comfortably hand-in-hand. They sang about the importance of believing in themselves and the power of personal accomplishment. They were smiling proudly and swaying together. In the end, one executive was particularly amazed at how good she felt. "I feel fulfilled, motivated, and rather free. I think before my board meeting tomorrow, I'll schedule some time for singing."

9. **Loyalty**: Imagine you are sitting at a steak house with a group of your peers. The steaks are served juicy, well-cooked, and delicious. Everyone picks up their knife from the table, except you. You reach into your pocket, take out a leather sheath, and pull out a special steak knife. "You brought your own?" you're asked. "You bet I did! I sell these knives. I believe in them and I refuse to use anything else! They're the best."

Pretty unusual, huh? Well, I was that knife connoisseur many years ago. One of my first jobs was selling knives, and everyone I worked with performed the same ritual. We carried our coveted steak knifes everywhere and when our food arrived, we proudly put them to use. Sure, we got strange looks and comments, but we didn't care. We firmly believed in our company and product and we were proud to express our dedication.

Aside from being a wonderful feeling, loyalty is a self-esteem enhancer. When we are faithful to a company, person, or even an idea, we feel proud because loyalty takes commitment, dedication, hard work, and integrity. Over the years I have heard many stories from people who found rejuvenation for their work or organization when expressing their loyalty.

Jack Walsh, of Nebraska, worked for a firm of about 500 employees. He wanted to get to know more people in his firm and feel a sense of community. That's why he got excited when he heard some employees were starting a club called The Optimists Panel, a forum for motivation and positive activities. Jack attended the first meeting and loved it. Even though there were only 15 in attendance, they were uplifting, warm, and well-rounded. They gave Jack the sense of community he was looking for.

After three meetings, Jack was still excited but began to feel frustrated because membership was not growing. He spoke up. "This is such a wonderful program. We've got to find a way to bring more people in. I'd like to try to get some major recruitment going."

Impressed and excited by Jack's enthusiasm, the members agreed to let Jack take on this endeavor and vowed to give him their full support. Jack devised a very clever marketing plan. Three weeks before the next meeting he posted eye-catching fluorescent posters all over the company that read, "See you at the T.O.P.!" Employees were curious. What is the T.O.P.? The next week he replaced those posters with ones that read, "The T.O.P. It's here and it's for you!" More gossip and whispers prevailed. Then a week before the next meeting, he replaced those posters with, "It's finally here. Discover the T.O.P. at ..." and he listed the date and time. The other club members helped by planning an extra-dynamic meeting, since they were anticipating a few more arrivals. They were wrong. There weren't a few extra people, there were 100! Jack's ingenious marketing plan worked.

Jane Hessler started her own consulting firm in the Midwest. In the beginning, she rented a small office, bought a computer, and hired only one employee, Helen Fredricks. At first, Helen's role was basically administrative: bookkeeping, answering phones, and setting appointments. As the business grew, so did Helen's excitement in watching the once small operation evolve into quite a company. Jane often told her, "One day we're going to be a household word. When you think of consulting, you'll think of us." "Us," Helen smiled. No one had ever made her feel so important and such a part of things. As time passed, Helen took on more responsibilities. She did some public relations work, contacting the media for articles, etc., and even made sales calls on slow days. She became so skillful that a company tried to recruit her, offering twice her salary. Though slightly tempted, Helen turned them down. She could never leave Jane.

Jane got a call one day from a firm in California. They wanted her company to relocate to California to be in charge of their account. They would fund everything: the move, office set-up, etc. The offer was perfect, except for one major thing; Helen felt it would be too detrimental to pull her children out of a school. Plus, her husband had just received a promotion. She didn't think she should go. Though heart-broken, Jane and Helen decided Jane should take the offer and they would stay in touch.

Jane loved California and her business was thriving, "But I miss you so much," she told Helen. "We'll team up again," the two women assured each other. Seven years after the move, Jane called Helen. "We just hit our first year in the million dollar range. I'm relocating to a larger complex and I need someone to keep the momentum coming. Nobody can hold a candle to you. Please think about it. It would be like old times."

Helen's kids were now entering college, and her husband was ready for a change, so she was delighted to tell her "yes." Jane held a party to honor her new employee. They laughed as they recapped the early days for everyone. "I'll tell you one thing," Jane told the group, "you never forget a wonderful team-player like Helen. I knew we'd join up again one day."

Joe Brozic and Tony Rogers, of Duluth, Minnesota, were only in high school when they discovered their loyalty to an idea. Joe was watching Madonna on T.V. and noticed that she was wearing many rubber bracelets. "That looks cool," he thought. "But I'd rather wear them around my neck." He shared his thoughts with his best friend, Tony, who agreed. Forming a partnership, the two young men approached 25 gift shops with their concept. Half laughed at their idea, and the other half supported it but said they'd only carry the product when the boys actually got it. However, they wouldn't help with the creation or funding.

After a long, hard search they found a manufacturing firm that could make it. Unfortunately, it would cost $50,000 to create the machinery to mold the plastic.

Joe and Tony didn't have that kind of money, but they had come this close — they couldn't give up. "There's got to be somebody that has this equipment," Joe declared. Thirty phone calls later, they found a firm in New York that already produced the rubber rings for some industrial equipment. "I'll sell you each ring at $.52 a piece." The deal was made. The shipment arrived and Tony and Joe priced the rubber rings at $3 a piece.

They started selling them at schools and got a huge response. Rubber necklaces had become the new fad. Soon they were selling them to gift shops and department stores. With the money they earned, Joe bought a new car and Tony put his money in a college fund. Role models for their school, Tony and Joe were invited to be guests at the entrepreneurial assembly so the other students could listen to their story and ask questions. One student asked, "Is being financially independent the greatest thing?" Joe and Tony smiled at each other. Joe answered, "Yeah. I'd be lying if I denied that, but the greatest thing of all is that after so many setbacks and rejections, we never gave up. I'm most proud of that. We're dedicated."

Whether it's a club, a partner, or an idea, dedicating yourself to something creates a tremendous sense of self-respect. I'm proud to tell you I still carry my knife with me. Sure, it's the most effective way to cut my steak, but it also reminds me of the importance of loyalty.

10. **Fun**: I recently saw George Burns, who is now in his late nineties, give his views on aging. When asked his secret to living so long, Burns replied, "Fall in love with what you do." Wise words. So many of us forget, or never realize, that our work can be pleasurable, exciting, and something we look forward to. This is important because most of us spend the majority of our lives working. People who spend that time in pain, dreading what they do, often end up bitter, stressful, and drained. If we spend that time loving what we do, we end up like George Burns: happy, fulfilled, and pleased to be nearing the young age of 100.

Obviously, it would be ideal to love every aspect of your work, and for some of us that is the case. But for many, we enjoy some parts of our jobs more than others. And finally, there are those who dread every aspect of their work day. In that instance, a drastic solution would be to change jobs entirely. Short of that, however, we can take the responsibility to find ways to make our work as interesting, meaningful, and as fun as possible.

When I was a manager for the knife company, one of my main duties was to run two-hour group information sessions to interested appli- cants. During our busy season, managers would have up to four of these two-hour ses- sions a day, often scheduling them back-to- back. I found myself feeling drained with this particular aspect of my job. After doing so many sessions, the zip that I initially felt for this task had fizzled. Needing to vent my frustra- tions, I called two other managers, Mark Bloom and Don Stucker, who ran territories nearby. They felt the same way I did. We all whined together, and then something unusual hap- pened. The more we talked about the sessions, the more we found humor in the whole thing. "We should make a video about it. It could be so funny," Mark added. And that's what we did.

The next day after work, we went to Mark's office. We scripted the skit as we went along and each of us took turns working the video camera. We all had different talents. Mark was hysterically sarcastic. He narrated the project with a David Letterman quality. Don was a physical comedian. He played different characters with an exaggerated edge. I added some creative touches to give the project extra flair. The one thing we all did well together was enjoy our production. Half the time we had to turn the camera off because we were laughing so hard.

At 3 a.m. we finished. The video was better than we thought it would be, and as far as the humor went, all of us laughed until we cried. "We've got to show this to all the managers. They'll love it," I said. So, we took the tape with us to the next managers conference a month later. A day-long session had ended and we asked the vice president if we could show the tape. Most people seemed like they wanted to go back to their hotel rooms, until they began watching. Their reactions were beyond our expectations. Some people fell off their chairs. Not only did everyone enjoy it, but they related to it. "Gosh, that was great," one manager said. "I thought I was the only one who suffered from sweaty palms, but when I saw you guys make a joke about yours, I felt so much better." Another manager said, "Thanks to you clowns, I'll never be able to do that informational session with a straight face again. Just when I was getting bored doing those sessions, you gave me a whole new way to look at it." Even the vice president had praise. "You three make the business so fun. We need more people to realize that they don't have to be so serious. A little enjoyment goes a long way." Making the video re-energized me. Even though other areas of my work were still stimulating, this one part had grown tedious. The video was just one way to bring some pleasure back into the process.

"You had fun cleaning up?" a friend asked her teenaged son who worked as a cook in a restaurant. Last year the woman and I were working on a project. Because of our busy schedules, we would often meet in the evenings at our homes. One night while we were going over work at the kitchen table, her 16-year-old came home from work. My associate had told me that she was very proud of him because he decided to work to pay for a stereo that he really wanted. She also found it amusing that he got hired as a cook because he hated doing anything in the kitchen at home. "He really works long hours and most of it is spent either over a hot stove or cleaning up after a long day. We'll see what happens." She was delighted to see her son's attitude was far more positive than she had expected.

That particular night, he walked into the kitchen looking a little unkempt. He was wearing his all-white chef's uniform, but you could hardly tell it was white because it was covered with stains. His hair was matted and messed up from his chef's hat and he smelled like salad dressing. While he may have looked disheveled, he obviously didn't feel that way. He gave us a big greeting, whistled his way to the refrigerator, pulled out a soda, and before he closed the door, spun around like a dancer and shut it. "Good day at the office?" his mother joked. He laughed and answered, "The best."

I was intrigued by his attitude and asked him what he liked so much about his job. "Well," he responded, "the job itself is kind of a drudge. I cook all day in a crowded kitchen and it gets really hot. Then, at the end of the day, cleaning up is a big project because everything gets so messy. But I really like it there because everyone makes it fun." I asked for further explanation. "Well, at the rush hours we make a game of getting the food out fast. We time ourselves and make contests out of it. That takes my mind off the pressure and turns it kind of into a sport. And clean-up is great because we have the restaurant to ourselves. We crank up the music and dance around and sing while we clean, plus we joke around a lot." "Sounds like fun!" I told him. "Your mother and I could use a little singing and dancing when we work." While I was joking, I really found his attitude inspiring. We could all take a lesson from this young man and learn how to make our drudge work amusing. You may not always love what you do, but you can sure make it a lot more fun!

11. **Self-Esteem**: Several years ago, I met a young man who, at the age of 25, set a goal to work so

hard that he could retire by the age of 40. "I don't want to spend my whole life working. I want to have freedom to do what I want," Ryan Hale told me. He was very intense about this commitment, so he set very specific goals on how to achieve it. He started his own business at 28 and built a very impressive home repair company. At 33, he was completely financially independent and bought his first home. Now he is 36 and when I tease him about retiring in four years, he laughs right back at himself. "Retire? I can barely take a week's vacation without going nuts. I miss the business. I don't know what I'd do if I didn't have my work. It's helped me feel so good about my life and myself."

Most of us complain about our work, but when we stop and think about it, our work really adds to who we are. The key word is "adds." Hopefully, you have found a great sense of confidence through your work. Since so much of our lives will be spent working, for the sake of a happy and fulfilling life, it is vital that our work makes us feel good about ourselves. For those people who feel their work "takes away" or destroys their self-respect or potential, they need to either find ways to improve their work situation or perhaps move on.

John Famer had studied long and hard to become a lawyer like his father and be a partner in the family practice. His father always said,

"Someday we'll work together. Father and son." Wanting to please his father, John naturally took that career path assuming it would make him happy, just like his father. John found law school fairly interesting, but once he passed the bar and became a lawyer, he felt very disillusioned. He disliked going over contracts and dealing with angry and hurt people. Most of his job involved conflicts, which was extremely uncomfortable for him. Despite his disdain for the work, he kept his position for over 10 years, never allowing himself to consider other possibilities for occupational fulfillment.

The turning point came in a rather ironic fashion. He was attending the retirement party for one of the firm's top officers, who got up to make a speech. The man toasted his company and colleagues and advised them, "I've been a lawyer here for over 30 years and I've loved every second of it. Life is too short. You've got to love what you do." These words throbbed in John's head like a beating drum. The more he listened, the more he faced reality. "I don't like what I'm doing." John took the next day off to spend a quiet day soul-searching. He realized that what he really liked to do was help and serve people in need. Even at the firm, his colleagues would comment on his overconcern for his clients' problems. After some months passed and John had checked out other careers, he decided social work would make him happy. He went back to school and became a social worker.

John finally realized that what was right for his father wasn't necessarily right for himself. He now had found something that was.

In the past several pages we have discussed many ways in which we can re-motivate ourselves in our jobs and our lives, but let us not forget the fact that there may be times to move on or make bigger changes. The key is to really listen to yourself and follow what you feel is right in your heart.

These personal motivational factors are a start to re-energizing yourself and your work. Every day, focus on one of these eleven points and create a purpose for yourself. Or perhaps you can take one point such as "Challenge" and focus on it for a month, rewarding yourself by finding a multitude of challenges on a daily basis. When we stop working on ourselves, we stop growing. It's up to you to tap into your motivation from within.

Another way you can use the previous list is to create more purpose and meaning to your work by making your own mission statement. Most companies have mission statements. Why not make your own? Take one of the words on the list of eleven and write your own mission statement. Nothing complicated or clever, just what hits home for you. Sample mission statements some of my seminar attendants have written are:

Today I will answer the phone as friendly as possible to create an atmosphere of high morale.

OR

I will accomplish as much as possible on a daily basis to be a role model for the people around me.

Now write yours.

MY MISSION IS _____

_____.

We all feel more valuable and worthy when we know our purpose. You can tape your statement up on your wall or just keep it in mind. Just remember, your attitude is where motivation begins and flourishes into action.

Before we conclude this chapter, I have three more tips to help you keep your confidence high.

1. Remember that personal esteem is something to be worked on every day, from the way you talk to yourself to the hobbies you choose.

Unfortunately, a lot of people either talk themselves out of improving their esteem or don't even realize that it can be worked on. An associate told me about a friend who unwittingly used language that affected his attitude and ability to take charge and grow.

A TV journalist that I know had recently started doing commercial voiceovers. After I heard him on the radio, I called to tell him how great he sounded. He thanked me and told me how much he enjoyed it and how well it paid, but then he surprised me with his last statement. "I wish I'd do them more often." What caught me off guard was the "wish." To me, to wish for something implies that we have no control — that the outcome of this wish has nothing to do with our own efforts. Do you wish to be thinner or do you take action to get there? Do you wish to be rich or do you take action to attain that goal? Sure, I sound picky and we all have used expressions that we don't literally mean, but what concerns me is that if we get used to using expressions that don't empower us, then we often tend to believe them. If I told myself a while back that I wish I'd start my own business, then I'm viewing my goal as a fantasy more than a possibility. However, when I declared that I'm starting a business, my language put me into an action state of mind.

With that thought, I said to my friend, "Why do you say that you wish you would do more when you can? Why don't you say that you are determined to do more?" I jolted him a bit. "You know," he began, "I honestly never thought about that. I guess I've gotten in the habit of using that expression. I never realized how it sounded or how it affected me." We talked for awhile about this idea and my friend began to search inside himself about some of his habits. He even said that maybe he was afraid to actually try to go after this new endeavor for all the reasons most people hold back in life: fear of failure, rejection, the unknown, etc. After taking a closer look at himself, he decided to start using more powerful expressions such as "I'm committed to," "I'm declaring that," "I'm dedicated to." Two months after our conversation, he had lined up five more voiceover ads.

The point is, improving ourselves takes hard work and also involves taking risks because changing is risky business. The other option, of course, is no growth, living in a rut, or simply just settling. But, change comes easier when you begin by committing to the smaller things first, such as quitting a bad habit like using disempowering expressions or negative self-talk. The journalist was an example of somebody who subconsciously talked himself out of expanding without actually realizing it at first. How many times have we all done that? We also talk ourselves out of growth by setting impossible standards.

I once worked on a project with two brothers who had a business together. They resembled each other, but one brother was very physically fit while the other had let himself go. The latter brother used to joke about this difference in a way that I felt was self-defeating. I pointed that out to him and he appreciated my feedback. In fact, he made the commitment right there to start an exercise program or stop talking about it. However, when I saw him a week later and asked him how the program was going, he was discouraged. "My brother has been doing this for a year. I'm so behind I'll never catch up with him."

You can see why he felt discouraged. By making his program a personal and seemingly impossible competition, he felt completely unmotivated. We talked about this approach and started setting realistic goals. The first thing we hashed out was that his plan should not have anything to do with his brother. Once he was able to accept this, then he set a reasonable plan that began gradually and advanced at a realistic rate. A month later, he was glowing. "How's the program," I asked. Without mentioning his brother he proudly declared, "I'm sticking to it and it's going fine. Now and then I cut my workout a little short, but I'm not going to punish myself. I'm going to keep trying." He felt capable of accomplishing the goals because they were planned in a way that was in line with his potential. Now, a year later, he is much more fit. He's lost 30 pounds, he eats healthy food, and he exercises regularly. Self-esteem can be continually enhanced with small steps.

2. Your grandmother was right! Stand up straight and smile. The more confidently you present yourself, the better you feel.

Sit up! Shoulders back! Don't hunch over! Throughout our childhood and teenage years we heard those demands from adults. Like so many teenagers, I resisted these requests for two reasons: (1) Naturally, I wanted to do the opposite of what I was told, and (2) I thought my elders were making a big deal over nothing. After all, why is posture such an issue? Then one day I was walking outside and I passed a window that caught my reflection. What I saw shocked me. I was hunching over so much that I looked tired and insecure. I stopped, put my shoulders back, held my head higher, and placed that imaginary book on my head. Lo and behold, I looked like an entirely different person — a vibrant and extremely confident one, if I say so myself. Posture is so important because the way we carry ourselves says much more than what we say or how we say it. Remember, 60% of communication is nonverbal. Again, people make assessments about us from, more than anything else, the visual image we project. And good posture and an infectious smile make all the difference.

3. Regardless of who you are or what you do, develop and use a strong, firm handshake. The first contact you have with people is through this ritual. If you let your fingers dangle, with no grip, you are making a statement. Conversely, a strong, firm grip says you like who you are. Good flirts shake hands quite well.

When I was recruiting during my days as a manager, I sometimes shook more than 50 hands a day. Like any other self-expression, I couldn't believe the diversity of handshakes. Some people barely grabbed the tips of my fingers, some squeezed so hard they almost crushed my bones, some people had nice firm grips, and some people offered limp fingers and palms. After shaking so many hands, I realized how much a handshake really says about someone. In fact, because I had such limited time to spend with each applicant, the handshake became a crucial element in my getting to know someone.

A limp and effortless handshake usually matched the person's personality. Then, there were people who grabbed my fingers rather firmly, but they didn't get my whole hand in there, web against web (the inside of your palm). One woman shook my hand that way, grabbing my fingers, and the message I received was that while she wanted to make an effort, she felt hesitant about her ability. During her interview she came across that way also: eager, yet not completely self-assured. When I met someone who squeezed my hand too hard, I could tell this person was nervous but willing to try. Sometimes people like that were overanxious, but I appreciated the effort and desire to impress.

The most appropriate handshakes, of course, are those from people who shake warm and strongly, with a nice, firm grip. They look you in the eye while doing so and you just feel their confidence. These people usually carry themselves the same way during an interview: self-assured, savvy in business, and approachable.

Betsy Frank, a petite vivacious woman I know, claims her handshake greatly helps her image. "My handshake has saved me many times. I'm short, I look much younger than I am, and I have a 'bubbly' quality, so I've been told. Often, when I first meet people, because of some of those elements, people make false assumptions about me. However, I make it a point to use a strong, firm handshake to eliminate any of those false impressions. Some have even commented to me, 'Wow, nice grip!' or 'You must be in sales.' My handshake allows me to declare my confidence."

We all have the chance to make a powerful statement about the way we feel about ourselves when we extend our hands. Use this tool to work for you. No matter what gender you are, occupation, or background, be the first one to extend your hand, make web to web contact, shake warmly and firmly, and look that person in the eye. Flirt for success. Within seconds, people will see how confident you are and you will see how confident you feel.

4

INTEREST IN OTHERS

"There are no uninteresting things
only uninterested people."

— Francois de la Rocherfoucald

Good flirts know this simple truth: All people are interesting. That's right. No two person's lives are exactly alike; no two person's opinions and views are exactly the same. And this means everyone has a story to tell. Sharing these differences is how we learn and grow. But as we all know, most people do not open up to each and every person they run across. There has to be a certain amount of trust. In other words, that interesting person needs to feel that you're interested in his or her story.

So, the question becomes, how do we show we are trustworthy and interested in others? By being an excellent listener. Sound too simple to be true? Well, yes and no. Anyone can learn to be a great listener, but it does take some effort. In fact, I've developed 10 keys to mastering the art of listening, which we'll explore here.

As you gain more insight into listening, consider this: Good listeners are so valued that people are drawn to them, are interested in them. And this two-way interest is bound to build the self-esteem of both persons. Sounds like flirting, wouldn't you agree? Now, on to the keys to effective listening:

1. Desire to listen.
2. Act like a good listener.
3. Stop talking.
4. Empathize.
5. Avoid distractions.
6. Communication takes responsibility.
7. Always respond positively.
8. Don't argue mentally.
9. Remember, we have different styles.
10. Make it fun!

Point #1. Desire to listen. This is where effective listening begins. Listening is an active, not passive, activity. That's why it takes true commitment. When we give someone our full attention, we need concentration and self-discipline. Like doing anything else, the first step then is to desire to do it.

Susan Grant told me about a gentleman in her company who apparently had no desire to listen. She and this man, we'll call Robert, were on a fundraising committee. Susan always thought

Robert seemed like a pleasant person when she'd pass him in the hallways, but in the committee, she saw a different side of him that disappointed her. Robert, like many others, did not listen. He constantly gave lengthy input during meetings, which was fine; however, when others wanted to speak, he either interrupted or completely ignored them by doodling or becoming lost in his own thoughts. His behavior disrupted the meeting's flow as members would find themselves having to say, "Just let me finish," upon being interrupted.

After three meetings, it became clear that everyone was perturbed by Robert's behavior. At the next meeting, before he arrived, someone joked, "Maybe Robert won't show up and I can get a word in edgewise." Everyone chuckled and talked briefly about Robert's annoying habit. Susan offered to confront Robert on his behavior in private and the group supported her. Not surprisingly, Susan's numerous attempts to explain this to Robert fell on deaf ears. He either claimed he was too busy to discuss it, or he'd belittle her by saying, "I'm listening at the meetings. I listen while I doodle."

Robert continued his rude behavior until something woke him up. At the end of one of the meetings, a member said, "Now let's recap today's meeting. Robert, why don't you help us out." Robert did so, only all he remembered was what he had said. When asked about John's theory on fundraising or Peter's idea on donations, Robert had no idea what was spoken. He was clearly embarrassed and seemed to finally begin to realize that he really didn't listen at all.

Robert was a different person at the next meeting. Most noticeably, he kept his mouth shut. He later told Susan that he almost interrupted a few times at that meeting, but strained to keep quiet, which was very difficult. However, once he really began to listen, he found himself enjoying the meeting. In fact, most people had wonderful ideas, some much better than his. He also noticed more. That Ginny had a delightful southern accent, and that Steve had a curious way of pronouncing certain words. He couldn't believe how much he had missed by hogging the floor and ignoring everyone else. In some ways, he was discovering new worlds, he said. Another thing Robert discovered was a warm feeling of respect and acceptance from others. It seemed that the more he changed, the more the committee members seemed to take to him.

Robert is just one example of somebody who learned to appreciate the benefits of listening. We all want to be valued, and to show how much we value others. Finding the desire to listen and making the commitment to do it is the first step to getting there.

Point #2. Act like a good listener. Have you ever heard of the adage "Act as if and the rest will follow"? That philosophy also applies to listening. When you take the proper stance of listening, it is nearly impossible not to listen because your body is so focused on the speaker that the mind usually begins to focus as well. Ways of acting like a good listener are: maintaining eye contact, leaning toward the speaker, shifting your whole body to face the speaker, nodding occasionally, smiling for encouragement when appropriate, and giving verbal encouragement such as "I see," "Umm. Umm," or "Fascinating." Indeed, good listening actions are so important that even when you may not be listening well, just by acting like an excellent listener, you make the speaker feel valued. This is not to say you should be insincere. But listening may require some time to start concentrating. By taking the initial "good listening" stance, you start the communication on a positive note, paving the way until you've adjusted to full focus.

Talk show host Arsenio Hall has mastered the body language of a good listener. Take note of his stance. Unlike other talk shows, Arsenio's set is staged in such a way so that there is no desk between him and his guests. He sits right next to them with no boundary between. Often, he moves an ottoman out of the way to get even closer. He usually leans in with his elbows on his knees to suggest immense concentration. And he places his jaw in his two hands with his index finger framing each side of his face. He also has immensely strong eye contact as he looks right into his guest's eyes. His nonverbal communication says he is listening and he makes his guests feel valued. We all could use his method.

Point #3. Stop talking. This point seems so obvious. How can we listen if we are talking? Though obvious, many of us have difficulty closing our mouths and letting the other person have the floor (so to speak) for awhile. We want to shout, "But, wait!" "I think ..." as soon as we feel passionate to speak. Yet, by interrupting we show a tremendous lack of respect, even a degree of immaturity. All it takes is commitment and understanding that while the other person is talking it is our job to be quiet, uninterruptive, and to listen. We all struggle with this. Just look at politicians who need monitoring and taming during a debate. It's up to us to show respect and monitor ourselves.

The notion of "stop talking" is also important to us as speakers. We need to pause throughout our explanations and stories to give our listeners time to give feedback, no matter how brief a pause. If we talk incessantly without taking time to give our listeners any room for comment, we alienate them. Again, we've all rambled on and on during stories, yet we need to be sensitive to our listeners and realize that they need to give occasional feedback and input even if we have "the floor."

Point #4. Empathize. This is such a necessary and useful concept to listening because it is the foundation of showing others that you understand. Empathy is defined as, *"Understanding so that the feeling, thoughts, and motives of one are readily comprehended by another."* When we feel that we are truly understood by another, we have an immediate

—

intimate connection and we trust him or her. In fact, that's the reason sales experts claim that empathy is a vital ingredient to successful selling.

One sales publication said, "salespeople simply cannot sell well without the invaluable and irreplaceable ability to get powerful feedback through empathy." Why is this? Because we understand people's needs and fears better by truly understanding their feelings. Good listeners and flirts express empathy and make the speaker feel valued and understood, causing the speaker to open up even more. Unfortunately, many people grew up in an era where discussing feelings was avoided and, therefore, understanding feelings was nearly impossible.

While discussing empathy in a communications workshop, Marla recalled, "I grew up in a family where empathy wasn't practiced. Instead, my parents used 'fix-it' statements. I remember when my first boyfriend broke up with me. 'Mom,' I said quivering, 'Steve just broke up with me.' I wanted to cry and talk about my hurt and know that it's O.K. to be sad. I needed to have my feelings validated. But my mom, with the best of intentions, used a different strategy, 'Don't worry, honey. You'll get a new boyfriend. There are plenty of fish in the sea.' She thought a cheer-up statement would help, just like her mom had taught her and so on. However, I felt even more confused and misunderstood. Logically I knew I would go on and someday find a new boyfriend, but emotionally I needed nurturing and comfort."

For good listeners, empathy is an essential ingredient. I am surprised at how difficult this concept is
for some people to grasp. I reviewed empathy for a
men's group and it took them a while to catch on,
but they got it. Perhaps that's because men have
been raised by society to be result-oriented versus
discussion-oriented. It seems that women have been
the gender which society looks to for nurturing,
emotional release, and support. But, we are all
capable of empathy. For most of these men, this
may have been a new concept. I challenged the
class to give me an empathy statement to this:

"Sorry I'm late gentlemen, but I had a car accident
on the way here."

The immediate responses were "fix-it" in nature.
Some included:

"I know a good mechanic!"
OR
"Well, at least you made it here O.K."

EVEN —
"Cars aren't that big a deal to repair."

While their efforts were commendable, not one
answer would have recognized my pain. Finally, one
man raised his hand with an eager smile. And in
one word he got the concept and expressed his
empathy eloquently.

"Bummer!"

"That's it!" I responded. "You understand empathy!"

Point #5. Avoid distractions. Good listeners know how to give their full attention and focus on the speaker regardless of the activity around them — be it phones, passersby, or any interference. It may sound easy to avoid distractions, but it's difficult.

In my seminars I ask participants to form teams of two. One partner is the speaker and is given a subject to speak about, as loudly as possible. The second partner's job is to listen as well as possible. I tell the listeners their job is important because after the exercise I will ask them to retell what they were just told by their partners. I also tell them to ignore me. The loudness during the exercise is distracting enough, but I also come around and talk in the ears of the listeners and drop papers in their laps. Knowing that they are going to be tested, the listeners usually do an excellent job. However, they strain to ignore my buzzing in their ear and struggle not to look at the papers. There's always the occasional partner who can't help but give these distractions a glance. Following this exercise, we have a discussion. One point that is always made is how this exercise simulates the office or even most every day life listening experiences. There are always phones ringing, people interrupting, or just general disturbances around us.

Now, we can't literally rid ourselves of these distractions, we must mentally rid ourselves of them. If we don't, we send the message to our speakers that we have no respect for them. That's the message I got from a supervisor years ago. On my first day, as he was training me, he stopped every few minutes to answer the phone or chat with a co-worker. Each time he let himself get distracted, I felt frustrated and less valued. I'm sure he had no idea of the message he was giving. How many of us do the same and we don't even realize it?

Point #6. Communication takes responsibility. Sometimes as listeners it is our job to guide speakers. As a very fast talker myself, I appreciate when a listener asks me to slow down or says he or she is having difficulty following me. I also appreciate when I'm told how well I am communicating with such remarks as "I understand," "I hear you!" or "Go on. Tell me more." Everyone needs feedback. As listeners, we should take a moment, without fully interrupting, to let speakers know how they're doing and how we're doing in receiving. Just a little bit of verbal and nonverbal encouragement can go a long way! And it's easy because it's natural.

During the previously-mentioned listening exercise where one person is assigned to speak and the other partner is assigned to listen knowing that he or she may be tested on the information, the listeners almost always assume they cannot say a word. They end up just looking at the speaker trying to take in all that is being said.

Following this activity I ask the group how it felt to be the listeners. The listeners, who thought they were not supposed to say a word during the exercise, usually say how uncomfortable they were. One woman said, "I had the urge to give feedback. It just felt so unnatural not to give any input at all to the speaker." Most of us would agree. As listeners we want to give some input, even if it is just "uh-huh." We want to let the speaker know that we are following the dialogue. How much of the responsibility should we take? Sometimes the amount even needs negotiation.

Marsha Grimm, of Oregon, told me about a time she negotiated this type of responsibility. "I was once on the phone with a colleague who, up to that point, I had only had brief conversations with. This particular time I was telling him a lengthy story. Half way through, I felt awkward because he hadn't said a word. 'Are you there?' I interrupted myself. He said, 'Absolutely. I'm listening.' I went back to the story and once again there was silence on the other end. 'Hello?' I said. My colleague explained the second time that he was listening. I believed him, but without any feedback from him, I felt alone. Finally, I told him what I needed. 'Tim, since I can't see you listening or nodding, I need to hear you. If you could every now and then give me an 'uh-huh' or an 'I see', it would really help.' I took the responsibility to help him learn what his role with me should be."

Conversely, if someone interrupts you too much, it's up to you to tell that person so. Sharing the responsibility of communication is a two-way street. As listeners, we need to take an active role in giving feedback to our speakers, and as speakers, we sometimes need to assist our listeners as to the type of feedback we need.

Point #7. Always respond positively. A television program featured several newspaper columnists discussing how they raise their children. One woman said that she wanted to instill as much confidence in her children as possible, and that's why when her six-year-old daughter told her that she wanted to be president one day, she responded with, "I'm proud of you, honey. That's a wonderful idea." The columnist went on to add, "I could have answered my daughter realistically with, 'Honey, we've never had a woman president and we may never have one. Is there anything else you'd like to be?' But I want her to have hope and personal belief. Even if I question the probability of her dream, I'm going to support her and help her believe in herself as much as I can."

I tell you this because, while this is not a book on parenting, we can all learn a lesson from this particular parent. How many times have we responded to someone's enthusiasm by "shooting down" his or her hopes?

When I started selling knives and told people what I was doing, the first thing I'd usually hear with a sarcastic tone was, "Oh, those ginsu knives? (Which they weren't.) No one will buy those. Sounds like a scam." They'd immediately jump to a negative conclusion and, in the process, distance me from them. Along the same lines, I once saw a co-worker tell her boss she was quitting the firm to follow her dream of being an actress. He said sarcastically, "Good luck. Only a million other people are trying to be stars also."

I am amazed and saddened by the lack of support I see people show one another. And the mind-boggling part of all this is that some people feel that the sooner they tell someone the "harsh reality," the more they help. How is blatantly destroying someone's hopes in any means helpful?

Human beings are delicate creatures. We all need hope, support, and positive feedback. And the moment we knock down aspirations, dreams, or ideas of others, we chip away at their self-esteem and distance them from us.

There is always a way to respond positively to people even if we don't necessarily agree with what they're telling us. In the world of flirting, responding positively is critical to keeping that rapport trusting and healthy. So, what do you do if a friend tells you he has this great idea to open a "scotch-tape only" store? While you may be tempted to say what a bad idea you think it is, no one's problems are "solved" with a dose of skepticism.

—

We help people when we show them that we believe they can solve their problems for themselves. Besides, the bottom line is people will do what they want to do. Remember, you can respond positively without agreeing. Some answers in this case could be, "That's an interesting idea. Tell me how you see it laid out?" or "That's a unique concept. Tell me about your marketing plan?" or even "Wow. I would have never thought of that. I like your taste for originality. Tell me, why scotch tape?" By responding positively, you keep his trust and show him you care. At the same time, by asking probing questions, you allow your entrepreneurial friend to sort out the details himself, and just maybe he'll come around to seeing your side.

"I have found the best way to give advice to your children is find out what they want and then advise them to do it."
— Harry S. Truman

Any good manager knows that the best way to empower employees is to help them come up with their own answers instead of telling them what to do. A top sales executive told me that when a sales rep complains that he or she is having a slump, she just says, "'Really? I'm surprised. What do you think it is?' Nine times out of ten, they have an answer. I'm just there to give support and congratulate them on finding their own solutions."

Teachers always remind students that there are no stupid questions. This is said so that no one is afraid to participate or ask about something. And it works. Imagine if Johnny raised his hand and asked what two plus two is, and his teacher said, "Dumb question, young man. We all know it's four." I doubt Johnny would ever raise his hand again. Well, every time we respond to someone with indifference or immediate skepticism, we create the same feeling.

We also need to address the notion of positive non-verbal responses. There is nothing better than talking to someone and watching him or her smile, nod, or show excitement. As a speaker, I am grateful for those audience members who give me those non-verbal expressions of support. A nod here, a smile there, and a laugh at the funny parts, makes all the difference. The more positively we can respond to others, the more positively they'll respond to us.

Point #8. Don't argue mentally. A group of executives from a marketing firm were at a meeting to discuss the company budget. The issue: where profits could be best reinvested. Susan Levin was up first to give her presentation, and John's turn was next. However, during the first few minutes of Susan's speech, John was so consumed with his own thoughts and why his plan was better, that he missed the details of her program. Lost in his head over this budget battle, John was flustered when he was called on to comment on Susan's outline. "Frankly," he mumbled, "I missed it."

It's easy to fall into the trap of focusing so much attention on disputing what the speaker is saying that we literally block ourselves from hearing anything but our personal thoughts. Our natural passion to disagree takes over. If this happens to us, we can remind ourselves that we won't forget our opinion. We don't need to disregard the speaker to sort our feelings out. Instead, we remedy this by training ourselves to listen as if we were going to be tested later. When our turn comes, we can state our argument verbally.

Point #9. Remember, we have different styles. We can't expect everyone to express themselves in the style that we choose. For example, I am a very verbal person. One of my associates is not as verbal. I remember a time we saw a training film together. Afterwards, we met another associate for coffee who asked us what we thought of the film. I ranted for literally half an hour, describing the concepts, directing, sets, etc. "Well, what did you think?" my film partner was asked. All she said was, "It was great!" What took me half an hour to describe may take other people three words. As a listener, patience is important. Everybody has a different style of communicating.

Stephanie Hamming, a writer, shared with me her experience regarding communicating styles. "Several years ago, I collaborated on a book project with a woman who communicated in a style much like mine. Sarah and I, in fact, used to joke about how similar we were. We both talked fast, we spoke loudly, we had a lot of energy, and we loved to analyze concepts. I enjoyed Sarah's partnership

immensely because, among other reasons, our simi-
larities made communicating easy and fun!

One day Sarah had told me about a woman she
met named Christie who was extremely knowledgeable about our writing topic. Sarah told me,
'Stephanie, you've got meet her. She is so intelligent
and extremely business minded. We can learn a lot
from her.' Trusting Sarah's judgement, I was anxious to meet Christie, and the three of us arranged a
lunch together.

In retrospect, I believe I imagined Christie would
behave like Sarah and I, since Sarah felt we would
all "click" so well. I was slightly mistaken. When I
met Christie, I was impressed. She certainly was
knowledgeable and helpful. At the same time, I was
frustrated. Christie communicated much differently
than Sarah and I. She talked very slowly. She took
long pauses to collect her thoughts and her energy
level was calm. When she would speak, I found
myself wishing she would speed up and pause less.
Basically, I wanted her to be like me. I wanted her
to communicate in a style that I felt more familiar
with. Throughout the lunch, I found myself fighting
her style. The calmer she was, the more enthused I
would be. If she was pausing, I'd try to prompt a
quicker response by breaking her thoughtfulness
with a leading question. Intentionally or not, I tried
to change her style to fit mine, which is not only
impossible, it's unfair. And the more I tried, the
more agitated I felt.

Sarah and I drove back together afterwards and she sensed my tension. I told her how I felt and she related, "You know, Steph, I felt that way, too, with Christie at first. Yet, once I decided to 'shift my gears', so to speak, instead of fighting her style, I enjoyed our communication much more." Sarah's input was wise. By combatting Christie's manner, I only made things worse for myself. So, I decided to shift as well. The next time we met with Christie, I focused on the positive attributes in her delivery, letting go of how I could make her be like me. Something miraculous happened. In my attempt to enjoy our differences, my style changed slightly. Whereas before I wanted Christie to speed up, now I concentrated on her pleasant, relaxing pace. I began to appreciate how poised she was and how peaceful her manner made me feel. And though she may not have talked fast, because her words were so well thought out, she always made effective points. After listening for awhile, I found myself mirroring her. Now I was slowing down, taking deep breaths, and thoughtfully pausing. And it felt good.

There's no way we can all communicate the same way, and that's fortunate. If we all sounded alike, behaved alike, and communicated alike, we'd be unchallenged and bored. The key is to accept our differences, appreciate them, and learn from them.

Point #10. Make it fun! This one is easy. Once you commit yourself to be an active listener, having fun is one of the best benefits. When we listen, we learn, we feel amused, challenged, surprised, etc.

etc. Listening can be fun in virtually any situation — whether it's a conversation with a stranger on a plane, a political speech, or a child's story about her day at school. There's no need to manufacture fun, it comes naturally. And all it takes is the commitment to listen effectively.

Now that we have covered how to show interest and flirt through active listening, let's move to an area where flirting may seem to be more of a struggle — negotiating.

In the opening of the book, we explored the notion that we all negotiate on a daily basis. However, for many of us negotiating creates conflict and tension. After all, doesn't negotiating mean two sides fighting for their own cause? Once again, adjusting our attitude can make us feel positive about taking on conflict or resolution. In fact, negotiating can be quite enjoyable once we know how to do it and realize it can be a win-win situation for all involved.

I became a fan of negotiating during my time as a saleswoman. As mentioned earlier, when I graduated from college I took a position with a direct sales firm: I sold knives. You can imagine how my parents felt knowing their naive 22-year-old was about to go into people's homes, many of whom were strangers, and try to sell knives. When I told my parents about my new position, they screamed and cried and I screamed and cried back. We definitely were not negotiating effectively. If I knew then what I know now, I would have never reacted that way.

Now I know how to negotiate effectively, and ironically it was the sales firm that taught me how.

What they taught me was something called a closing cycle, which I have renamed the Negotiating Cycle. It has improved my communication skills immensely and worked for hundreds of my seminar attendants. I am going to share it with you. What you may find is that you have been a master negotiator your whole life without even realizing it. First, I will share the formula with you, and then we will use it in a number of scenarios.

THE NEGOTIATING CYCLE

(Step 1) AGREE

(Step 4)
ASK AGAIN

(Step 2)
AND or AT THE
SAME TIME
BUT or HOWEVER

(Step 3) LOGIC

For the first scenario, I will use my experience as a knife saleswoman to show how each step works. I have just done my sales presentation for Mrs. Smith, who loves the knives and would like to purchase them, but she feels hesitant because "knives just aren't a priority." I respond by starting with Step 1 — agreeing. "I agree, Mrs. Smith, and I can understand how you feel. I never think of knives as a priority. I'd much rather spend my money on clothes or cars or food."

Before I continue with the cycle, imagine how this response made her feel. I showed her that I understood her point and therefore we are now on the same level, creating trust and receptiveness. That would not have happened if I had responded by disagreeing and saying, for example, "That's not true, Mrs. Smith. Knives are a priority whether we want to believe it or not because we eat at least three times a day and spend more time in the kitchen than any other room." Even though my logic may be true, by disagreeing with her from the outset, I'm creating a righteous tone and creating a mood of defensiveness. By agreeing with her first, I set a tone of understanding and comfort, and therefore my logic will be accepted in a non-threatening way.

Next comes Step 2, which is a transition into Logic. You'll notice on the negotiating cycle model that I've crossed the words "But" and "However" out, as their usage would seem to negate the agreement I just made with Mrs. Smith. Listen to the difference. "I agree that I don't view knives as a priority, but we are in the kitchen at least three times a day and will be the rest of our lives." The "but" discounts my first statement. Examples: "I really like you, but I just want to be friends." "I will pay you back, but I just need more time."

Every time we use "but" when dealing with people's feelings, we wash away any positive reasoning we began with. The more we can effectively set and maintain a tone of understanding, the more relaxed and trusting our dealings will be. By simply taking the "but" out of our statement and replacing it with something less defensive, we keep the tone in a receptive arena.

"I agree that knives may not be a priority. At the same time, we are in the kitchen at least three times a day . . ." The transition makes a comfortable space for a logic statement, which continues, "and we will be in the kitchen for the rest of our lives. That's what's so great about these knives. Since they're guaranteed forever, you buy them only once so that they never have to be a priority again. Then we can turn our financial focus on items we really want like food, clothing, entertainment."

Now that I have pointed to the logical side, in a gentle way, I can move on to Step 4 — asking again, "So you can see why purchasing this set today makes sense in the long run, Mrs. Smith?" I am comfortable asking for the order again because I know that Mrs. Smith feels understood and because I presented my logic in such a way that assists her in looking at the situation differently without attacking her.

Once I understood this negotiating cycle and used it, I actually looked forward to negotiating because it showed my customers that I was coming from a place of concern versus righteousness or pressure. In fact, this cycle works effectively in most negotiating situations, and you may have been using it your whole life without even realizing it.

Let's look at another scenario. Many of us have teenagers (and we've all been teenagers). This situation may be familiar. Let's say a teenager wants to borrow the car, even though he has been justly grounded and forbidden to use it. By using the negotiating cycle, our teenager (let's call him Eddie Haskell, for fun) can effectively present a win-win situation:

Eddie: Mom, can I borrow the car tonight?

Mom: No, Edward. You know you're grounded.

Eddie: **Step 1 — Agree.** You're right, mom. I deserve to be grounded and not have the car since I stayed past my curfew last week. I'm glad you and dad showed me the errors of my way.

Step 2. At the same time ...

Step 3 — Logic. ... if I don't borrow the car, then I can't get to my final exam. If I can't get to my final exam, then I'll fail this class. If I fail this class, then I'll fail school and have to live here with you and dad forever.

Step 4 — Ask again. So, can I just borrow the car to get to my test?

If Eddie had begun negotiating by arguing, "Mom, c'mon. You've got to let me have the car," he would have created tension. By agreeing at the outset, even in his "Leave It To Beaver" sarcasm, he prepared his mom to listen to him.

The great thing about the negotiating cycle is that it is merely a recreation of the flirting principles we have already discussed. Step 1 — agreeing is showing EMPATHY. When you agree, you show your negotiating partners that you hear and understand their feelings. They want to continue doing business with you because they see that you care. Step 2 — using "at the same time" instead of "but" expresses your support even further. Your "agree and" shows that though you may bring new logic into the equation, you are still validating their feelings, whereas "but" would take them away. Step 3 and 4 — using logic and asking again are related to our discussions on CONFIDENCE and ENTHUSIASM. When you believe in yourself and your product or service, you can present your ideas in a sincere and positive way.

One of my seminar attendants used this cycle to negotiate her way into a sold-out concert. She told me, "When I got to the door of the small club for the concert, I treated the ticket person with respect and compassion. At the same time, I re-expressed my confidence in my plea to be let in. When she told me the concert was sold-out and that she couldn't let me in, I said, 'I can understand how you have to do your job. I've worked places where I had to turn people away even when I didn't want to. And you've probably been in my shoes, too. I have tried every way I know how to get tickets. They were being sold while I was away. This is my favorite singer and I would do anything to get in. Is there anything I can do to get in for just a while?' She did understand where I was coming from and told me her 'locked out of concert' story. After we talked for a while, we came to a compromise. She said the bouncer was her friend and I could go in only if I stood with the bouncer in the back and stayed there. I was more than happy with this agreement and sincerely thanked her, telling her she made my night. 'Well, at least somebody here appreciates me,' she said with a smile."

There is a moral here. People like to negotiate and help others out, especially when they know it's appreciated. Remember PEOPLE DON'T CARE HOW MUCH YOU KNOW UNTIL THEY KNOW HOW MUCH YOU CARE.

This negotiating technique also works effectively on the phone, even without the advantage of eye contact. Two extra points to stress here are to try to use names to create a sense of intimacy, especially since we don't have the advantage of seeing the other person, and make sure you thank people sincerely. Here's how I flirted and negotiated with a customer service rep of a phone company and had a problem handled immediately.

Rep:_____ telephone company. This is Vera.

Jill: Hi, Vera! My name is Jill.

Vera: Oh, hi! (She seemed surprised and happy I offered my name.)

Jill: I need your help. I had my business service installed yesterday and it's not working. I'm nervous because I may be missing valuable calls, which could really hurt my company. Has there been a mistake? Or maybe I'm confused about how this works. (I expressed that I was counting on her, and I maintained my composure without using blame or anger.)

Vera: Well, actually maybe you weren't informed, but the service takes three days to start after installation.

Jill: Oh, I see. I wasn't aware of that. Perhaps I misunderstood. Anyway, that puts me in a bind. I have some very important calls coming in this afternoon and I have to leave for an appointment. Vera, I need to get those calls answered. What can I do? If you help me here, I'll be indebted to you forever! ("Need her" expressed urgency versus "Can you help me?")

She laughed at my desperate humor and said she'd see what she could do immediately. She also gave me her direct line and told me to sit tight until she figured something out. Fifteen minutes later, she called with a solution. I could use a temporary answering system until mine started. I could tell she was excited to solve my problem. I thanked her many times and told her she had given the phrase "customer service" a new-found respect in my eyes. We joked for awhile about other phone disasters. By the time I hung up, I felt I had made a friend. Now, whenever I am having trouble with my system, I call right through to Vera.

The story with Vera shows that phone flirting can get the same results as in-person flirting. Here are four tips to effective phone flirting:

FOUR TIPS TO PHONE FLIRTING

1. **Always sound enthusiastic when answering or receiving a call.** Remember, since you don't have the ability to see the other person, your tone of voice becomes the single most important factor in the impression you are making. When you answer the phone, if you are receptive, the person on the other end feels motivated to continue and naturally mirrors your enthusiasm.

Barney Richmond, of Dallas, told me about an incident where simple phone enthusiasm clinched a decision for him. "I once had an important business engagement and needed a suit I had recently purchased tailored. Since I had just moved to Texas, I didn't know any good tailors so I turned to the phone book. The first companies I called were the ones with recognizable names or had large ads. I figured they were reputable.

"On my first call, the receptionist was pleasant, but she put me on hold for so long that I hung up and called back. I explained what had happened and she said she'd try again. Once again, I was holding for an unreasonable time, so I moved on. The next place I called didn't put me on hold, but they were rude. The person who answered sounded cold and irritated over having to give information on rates and location. My third call went to a company that only had one line in the phone book — no large or fancy ads. 'Thomas' Tailors, this is Susan!' This was the warmest and most personable greeting I had heard so far. When I asked about rates and other details, Susan said she'd be glad to help. After answering my questions, I learned that Susan was the receptionist, the bookkeeper — and the tailor. She was a one-woman operation. I liked her right from the start. She had given her name immediately, which made me feel like I was talking to a human being. The other places made me feel like I was talking to a robot. Moreover, she was friendly and obliging throughout our conversation, and though her shop was not as convenient as the other places I had called, I happily gave her my business."

So far we've discussed the manner of people who answer the phone. How about when you are the caller? Remember, your cheerfulness is vital because you are not only making an impression, you are setting the stage for positive communication.

Peter Freeman, a sales manager I met at a convention, told me about one of his sales reps, Ben, who had an amazing ability to get appointments from cold calls. Over the phone Ben came across with excitement, sincerity, and an infectious sense of humor. One day, he called Peter at the office to tell him he had been in a car accident. Though he and his car were fine, he felt drained and decided to reschedule his last appointment. "I'll go home and schedule more sales calls for next week," Ben told Peter. That night, Ben called Peter again. He sounded tired and distressed, not like himself at all. He told Peter he had called five people and couldn't set up one appointment. Ben was confused. "This is so unusual for me. I haven't even changed my pitch. I can't figure it out." Peter asked him how he felt he sounded during his calls and Ben told Peter he sounded like he does now. "I just don't have the energy I usually do because the accident threw me for a loop." The two men agreed that it was better that Ben try tomorrow. The next day he called Peter. Ben was back, his enthusiasm was again present, and he had good news to report. "Six out of six setups!" Though Ben didn't change the words of his sales pitch, his tone of voice had changed, and that's what had hindered his success.

Think about it, we mirror each other on the phone. If you call someone who, because of their environment, needs to talk at a whisper, even though you are in a different location where noise is permissible, you tend to whisper as well. Therefore, if you call with positive expectancy, you'll get positive feedback. And finally, keep in mind that since so many people's jobs involve long hours on the phone, they may feel frustrated with the negative tone of previous callers. Make sure your call is the "pick-me-up" they may need by being enthusiastic and friendly. An associate once called a busy television newsroom to try to get a story on. The first thing she said was, "Hi! I'm Susan Conson. I have a great story and I'll be brief because I know that you are so busy." What Susan heard on the other end was a surprisingly warm, "Sue, we love you already. We appreciate briefness here." Call with respect, you'll get respect.

2. **Learn the name of the person on the other end and use it.** Dale Carnegie once wrote, "Remember that a person's name is to that person the sweetest and most important sound in any language." Using names is such a powerful flirting technique because it creates an immediate sense of intimacy. Imagine you are talking to Doug. He asks you how your day was and you respond in one of two ways. Read the two responses out loud and notice the difference in the impact:

"I had the worst day"
OR
"Doug, I had the worst day."

Notice how much more intimate the second response sounds just by adding one word — Doug's name. When we use people's names in conversation, we make them feel important and that we are truly trying to connect with them. This is especially vital on the phone where you don't have the benefit of direct eye contact.

Earlier, you read about a tailor who answered the phone, "... this is Susan." By stating her name at the outset, she opened up the opportunity for intimacy. By telling callers her name, they feel free to tell her theirs. For example, "Hi, Susan. My name is Jill. I'm calling about ..." Within moments, the disclosure of our names make us feel more like friends. Have you ever noticed that when you call directory assistance operators they answer by giving their names? "Directory assistance. This is Andy. How can I help you?" At that point, we can just tell Andy what we need — "I need the phone number to the weather." Or we can take Andy up on his subtle offer. "Hi, Andy. I'm Jill. I need the number to the weather." Which response do you think would most likely get better service?

When people offer their names upon answering the phone, use it! They are opening the door to bonding, and by not using that name or offering ours, we are shutting the door. So, what do you do if the person doesn't give his or her name? Offer yours first.

When I call a company, let's say Trend Setters, and someone answers, "Trend Setters ...", it is up to me to create a sense of bonding. "Hi! My name is Jill Spiegel. I need to inquire about rates. Are you the person I should be speaking with?" No matter if they are or aren't, we need to say, "Oh, thanks, and what is your name?" Then I can use the person's name immediately. "Well, thanks, Dave, for all of your help. You've been great!" Now if I ever call Trend Setters again, I have a friend there.

Every time you learn a person's name at a company, write it in your records so you won't forget. When you call back a month later and remember Dave's name, good service is almost guaranteed and a more solid rapport has been built.

Before we move on to the next point, keep in mind that using names is powerful as long as it's done tactfully. Has this ever happened to you? I had a telemarketer call me this week who used my name to an exaggerated degree. It sounded something like this:

"Hello, Jill. The reason I'm calling, Jill, is to tell you, Jill, about a great service our company is offering. Now, Jill, ..."

Obviously, this turned me off. It was like getting a form letter with my name repeatedly stamped in it. In that case, hearing my name felt awkward because the approach was phoney. Once again, the key is sincerity. Use names appropriately and that person on the other end will like you, give you better service, and probably remember your name too!

3. **Call during receptive times.** Have you ever arrived at work on Monday and felt like you were in a fog? No matter what you do, you just can't shake it. Then comes a call from someone who is interested in negotiating. "Ugh. I can't deal with this right now," you think. We all have certain times, and days of the week, where we just feel more "on," or alert, than other times. As a caller, it's important to be aware of that fact. Again, when it comes to phone flirting, since you don't have the advantage of face-to-face contact, other aspects become more important, and one of them is timing.

If you are calling a business to either make a contact or sell a service, Mondays, and even Tuesdays, may be tricky. People are just getting in the flow of their work week and may not feel quite as receptive as later in the week when they've not only got momentum, but feel enthused, sensing the weekend ahead. So, calling on Wednesday or, even better, Thursday will give you a greater chance of catching people in an open frame of mind. Calling Fridays, though, the last day of the work week, can be less effective because many people are more focused on the upcoming weekend than getting business done. (On the other hand, if you want to reach the president of a large firm, he or she is most likely the last one to stay on Friday.)

In addition to days of the week, times of the day can also be important. Beware of the first thing in the morning. People need to settle in, have their coffee, check their messages, etc. Eleven o'clock is a good time to call as most people are "in the flow" of their day and lunch is just ahead. Right after lunch is a bit premature. Again, people need time to adjust. Two thirty to four o'clock are effective call times. The afternoon has taken course and the end of the day is just around the corner — most people are in a good mood.

Finally, when it comes to the notion of time, most importantly we need to respect the time of others. When we call people, though it might be a good time for us, it may not be for them. Let the person know you are aware of that by asking courtesy questions such as, "Is this a good time?" "Are you in the middle of something?" "Do you have a few minutes?" Or you can handle it assertively with time-respectful statements such as, "I'll be brief. I know you're a busy person. This will just take a second." When you appreciate other's schedules, they appreciate you.

4. Use the words "I need" versus "can you." I need you to read this next paragraph. Could you possibly read this next paragraph? Which statement in the above sentences is more likely to call you to action? The first one. People, whether in-person or on the phone, respond to urgency. When we call a company for assistance, our chances of getting help are a lot better when you sound urgent by using the words, "I need you to ..." When we make statements such as, "Could you maybe help me ..." or "Do you think you could ...", we sound doubtful. A hesitant tone suggests you don't expect results and, therefore, the person on the other end is unlikely to help you.

Many years ago, I needed a rental car as soon as possible. I called four places and began my pitch with, "Do you think you could rent me a car?" Every place said they were booked and apologized. I called two other places whose lines were busy, which made me agitated, so I called the first company again and this time my tone was desperate. "Hi! I need a rental car as soon as possible." The same woman answered the phone who had answered the first time, but she didn't recognize my voice (I hadn't learned the power of using names yet). This time she was more receptive. "Well, right now we're booked, but let me see what I can do." I flirted more. "Thank you so much. I'm in a terrible situation and I really need your help. I'll owe you my life!" I kidded. She laughed, put me on hold for a few minutes, and came back with her answer. "I

located a car. You can have it within the hour."
She seemed just as relieved as I was.

When we tell people we need them, we flatter
them. People really do like to help. When you
show people you are counting on them, they
don't want to turn you away. Remember, this
strategy is suitable for certain situations more
than others. If you are selling a car, saying "I
need you to buy this car" is, of course, inappro-
priate. However, if you are calling a company to
reach a certain person, it is O.K. to tell the
receptionist you need help. The key is to use
common sense. Phone flirting becomes more
natural and less technical when you put yourself in the other person's shoes (or perhaps I
should say when you put yourself on their end
of the line).

5

RAPPORT THROUGH COMPLIMENTING

"Flattery will get you anywhere"

My mother and I had a running joke every time I came home to visit from college. I'd walk in the house, see my beautiful mother, and tell her how great she looked. She would respond with, "You can have whatever you want for dinner. Flattery will get you anywhere." She was kidding; or was she?

As a key to successful flirting, I have stressed that the better you make others feel, the more they trust you and the greater the chance of getting your business or negotiating goals accomplished. So far, we have discussed several ways to show people that you care: listening actively, having a sense of humor, asking questions, etc. This chapter is dedicated to showing others that you care through COMPLIMENTING.

While any sincere compliment is a good compliment, some compliments are more effective than others. Below is a list of effective styles of complimenting and even more effective complimenting strategies. After we take an overview, we'll explore each point in depth.

Effective	More Effective
Stay away from general words such as "great" or "nice"	Use specific language such as "dynamic" or "warm"
Avoid focusing only on the obvious	Focus on more hidden subtleties
Don't overfocus on outside appearance	Focus mainly on internal attributes
"Good Job" needs explanation	Tell how this "Good Job" was extraordinary

Jamie Lewin found herself getting irked by her colleague and long-time friend every time she'd pay her a compliment. "You look nice, Jamie," she'd say. Or, "Your outfit and hair look nice together." One time Jamie finally snapped, "Nice!? Tammy, what do you mean by nice? The couch looks nice and so does the carpet! In what way do I look nice?" Jamie was frustrated because she needed specifics. What exactly was it that made her hair and her outfit go together so well? We all crave to hear specifics because it makes us feel that the compliment is truthful and sincere. Certainly, Tammy meant well with her words of praise. Yet, Jamie found her expressions "meaningless." Anyone can say anything is nice. Jamie wanted to know what was so "deep down" special.

It's easy to fall into this trap of making general compliments. Early this fall I did a seminar for a college fraternity. I was so impressed with the gentlemen of this organization. "You were all so nice!" I told the fraternity president. He seemed disappointed. "I get that all the time," he said. "How nice I am. I don't know why, but it makes me feel funny." I tried a more specific approach later in the day. "Everyone made me feel so welcome. The minute I got off the plane you made me feel like a good friend." His face lit up. This time the compliment had an impact. "That really makes me feel great. We all work hard to make people feel a part of the fraternity when they work with us. I'll pass that on to the guys."

Specific compliments usually strike people as more sincere than general ones. When people give us compliments in detail, we tend to believe and trust them more. There's proof behind their flattery. We can tell they really have noticed.

Ann Trent told me about one compliment that made a difference with her. She explained, "I once wore a new suit to a club that I attend weekly. I remember receiving several compliments on my suit, such as 'You look great,' 'Nice suit,' and 'Wow!' Of course, all of these comments were pleasing. Yet, the one that really struck me came from a woman who said, 'Wow, Ann. That blue suit against your dark hair has a dynamic impact. You really look like the true professional today!' This particular comment felt more sincere to Ann because she now had a reason that explained what made her look so special that day.

Giving specific praise also gives people realistic expectations. Most parenting books stress that when complimenting children, give them specific terms that they can work with. After all, what does the "best" mean? How can anyone improve from there? In addition, children know the "best" is often impossible to reach, so the term can sound dishonest. Specific compliments are truthful and realistic. Telling a child that they colored in the lines even better on this drawing than the last one is a lot more effective than telling them they drew the nicest picture you've ever seen. The same philosophy can be applied to adults. You can tell someone his haircut looks great, or you can tell him his new haircut looks great because it really frames his face.

While detailed compliments makes sense, it can be difficult to find the right words because when giving people praise, we often instinctively think in superlatives: Wonderful! Terrific! Nice! Great! The easiest way to avoid this trap is to tack on the word "because" every time you make a general statement. This will help you draw out specifics. For example, after a colleague of mine made an excellent speech, I told her, "It was great!" I immediately tacked on, "Because you had strong eye contact with the audience and your personal stories were moving."

Even replacing common expressions such as great, nice, wonderful with more descriptive adjectives can make a compliment more sincere. A "great" speech can also be a powerful, moving, or captivating. A nice person can also be thoughtful, caring, and good-hearted. Now, tack on the word "because" after those adjectives and you've really got a meaningful compliment.

1. "Jane, you're a nice person."
2. "Jane, you're a thoughtful person."
3. "Jane, you're a thoughtful person because you always take the time to do the little things that make me feel special."

Moreover, with a sincere compliment like that, you not only make the person feel appreciated, you also learn why you appreciate that person, which helps you feel that much more sincere.

Stacey Blatt, a former spokesperson for a home-shopping network, told me how specific compliments helped her sell merchandise on TV. She explained, "Most of the items were various types of jewelry — all of it beautiful. Now if I had said every piece was beautiful or pretty, I would have been a poor saleswoman. After all, the same description becomes boring after a while. It was my job then to find reasons why the items were beautiful or why somebody would like them, in order to show the viewers why each item was unique. At first, I thought this would be difficult, yet I found it was actually fun and enlightening. A bracelet was no longer just pretty, it was festive and playful — something that would put me in the mood to go to a party. A beautiful ring became an item that made me feel elegant and had the tone of richness and royalty. A heart pendant necklace was more than attractive, it was soft and romantic and something I could give to myself as a gift of love to me. It was my job to sell these items and in order to sell, I needed to come across sincerely. Getting descriptive about these products helped my selling ability because I convinced myself, not just the audience, of the qualities of each item."

Take a moment and try it yourself. Take your favorite piece of clothing and give it a sincere compliment:

This _____is great because_____.
OR
My best friend is wonderful because_____.
OR
My favorite restaurant is _____because_____.

Specific complimenting is easy if you just remember to be sincere. The more you practice using specific language, the easier it becomes. In fact, you'll probably find yourself paying many compliments to close friends and acquaintances. Later, we'll discuss what rewards you get back.

Avoid focusing on only the obvious; focus on hidden subtleties. Our next guide to complimenting also stresses the importance of sincerity. When we always comment on obvious positive traits, we have less impact than if we notice more hidden subtleties. For instance, I'm often told how bubbly, energetic, or enthusiastic I am. I was born with a naturally upbeat quality and most people choose to focus on that characteristic when complimenting me. While I certainly appreciate that warm feedback, it sometimes feels less powerful than other compliments I've received.

For instance, I just attended a wedding where I made a speech for the 200 guests. Subjecting myself to so many people, I was happy to hear the praise after the speech. The majority of comments I heard were about my energy. People definitely saw the obvious. But, the two pieces of feedback that struck me went beyond my apparent external qualities. One person said how my story really flowed and the punchline at the end came unexpectedly, adding to the humor. The other piece of feedback that stands out in my mind was about my memory. During my speech, I mentioned the names of several of the new guests I had met. I had worked hard to remember their names. So, when this person commented on my memory, I was flattered that someone had truly listened to my speech and thought about my effort. The more others notice the hidden "little things," the more they show their sincerity.

Think about yourself. Was there a time or times in your life where you felt especially flattered because someone took the time to notice something about you that wasn't too obvious? This same concept applies to our third rule of thumb in complimenting:

Don't overfocus on outside appearance; focus mainly on internal attributes. "You look beautiful today!" "Wow! Where did you get your hair done?" "What a gorgeous outfit. It's so flattering on you!" It is easy to compliment on externals because those features are the first things we see when talking with someone. Alex, my cousin, always takes time to dress extra creatively. I comment on her latest self-made style every time I see her at family holidays. After I caught myself marveling over an outfit for the fifth Thanksgiving in a row, I decided it was time to let her know I appreciated her deeper qualities as well. (We'll get to that compliment in a moment!) The point is, if we always compliment looks, we send a subconscious message that appearance is most important to us, or that the way someone looks is linked to the way we value them, which can often be a dangerous and unhealthy message.

Again, let's refer to parenting. If you only praise children for their cute smiles or adorable looks, you tell them that is what's most important. An associate of mine learned through extensive therapy that her eating disorder was linked to her childhood because she was praised so much for her attractive appearance. She became obsessed with looking perfect, feeling that brought her love and approval.

We also need to pay attention to the messages that we send to adults. By learning to focus on exceptional internal qualities, we appreciate people for who they truly are. Anyone can get a new haircut, change an outfit, or get a tan, but it is the inner qualities that are our true gifts and make us who we are. I am not suggesting that you never compliment people on their appearances, but mix those comments with internally focused ones. Moreover, have fun mixing these two types of compliments together, which is what I did when I altered my compliments to Alex.

Upon seeing Alex at the most recent holiday, once again I noticed her creative outfit. This time when praising her, I made her outward appearance a reflection of her inner qualities. "Alex, your flair for changing style says so much about you. You've always been so adventurous and daring, which is one of the reasons I love to be with you."

An entertainer I once worked with also did a wonderful job of mixing externals and internals when he complimented another speaker. "Laura, you give off so much happiness when you speak. Even your eyes sparkle." While he flattered Laura on her sparkling eyes, he helped her see that this feature was a reflection of what she had within. I saw the same method of praise work during a flirting seminar. People were told to pay a heartfelt compliment to their partners. One man's face lit up when his partner said, "I really like your suit. I noticed it as soon as you sat next to me. But now that I've gotten a chance to know you better, I see that the suit is a great representation of how you come across: bold, organized, and dynamic."

This type of complimenting is a fun personal challenge. Next time you find yourself praising someone on his or her externals, test your creativity by turning the remark into an internal focus, for yourself and for the compliment receiver. Who knows? "You have a great smile," could evolve into, "Your smile is contagious. People around you always seem to be in a better mood."

Our final tip on effective complimenting also deals with sincerity:

"Good Job" needs explanation; tell how this "Good Job" was extraordinary. This idealogy actually comes from a time in kindergarten when I made a Mother's Day card. Each of us made a colorful, elaborate card on which we were instructed to complete, in our words, the answer to this question: "I love my mother because . . . "

Some of the answers included, "She makes the best peanut butter and jelly sandwiches," "She helps me feed my dolls," "She is silly," "Even when she's tired she reads me a story." All of us like to feel we are good parents, but hearing specifically what really makes us special as a parent is some of the best reassurance we can ask for.

Now think about this theory when complimenting a boss or co-worker. If you are in a supervisory position, for example, hearing from a staff member that you "are a great supervisor" can make you feel good. But you also know that it is your job to be an effective supervisor, so in a sense being a great supervisor might mean that you are simply doing your job. You want to know what makes you extra-effective as a supervisor. "As a supervisor you are such a positive role model. The way I see you make your family such a large part of your life shows me how important and possible it is to have balance in my life."

When an associate of mine recommended that I use her financial advisor, she said, "Jill, you've got to call Jim. As I told him last week, he's more than an accountant, he's a therapist. He knows that money can be such an emotional matter so he deals with his clients' needs and feelings as well." For that comment alone, I did call on Jim to handle my finances. I knew he did his job extra effectively. Let's face it, I'm sure General Schwarzkopf would enjoy being told he is a great leader. But, in one of my flirting class exercises, we took this compliment one step further by explaining what makes him extraordinary. "You're a great leader because in addition to knowing how to lead, we can tell that you have much compassion and concern for the men and women on your team."

Part of the fun in learning how to compliment effectively is knowing that you can find something positive and sincere to say to just about anybody.

Here are some examples from my flirting seminars:

DONALD TRUMP

Effective:	**More Effective:**
"Boy are you rich!"	"Your financial success shows how determined you are."
"It must be great to be surrounded by so many beautiful women."	"Even with your personal life in the tabloids, you are still so composed and focused."

CHER

Effective:	**More Effective:**
"You have a great body!"	"I respect the discipline you have to stay in such healthy shape."
"You do great infommericals."	"You have a natural sales ability that's casual and convincing."

Indeed, complimenting can definitely be an art form. And the more you feel that you do it well, the more you'll find yourself doing it!

But why should we compliment? There are several reasons. One reason may seem obvious and one that we have discussed throughout this book. A large part of building rapport involves appreciating others and making them feel good about themselves. Sincere and effective complimenting is one way to achieve this. The second reason may not seem so obvious. Complimenting others is also a way to make ourselves feel better. Mark Twain once said:

THE BEST WAY TO CHEER YOURSELF UP IS TO CHEER SOMEBODY ELSE UP.

When you pay someone a heartfelt compliment, you watch his or her face light up, you see a smile where there previously wasn't one, and you often see an expression of pleasant surprise: "Wow! Someone noticed." Corny as it sounds, it feels good to make others feel good. Try it next time you're having a somber day or things don't seem to be going well. Turn your attention from your problems and take a moment to pay a compliment. It makes you feel much better.

Janet Brandy, who works for a graphic arts firm, told me about an experience that taught her the power of complimenting. She recalled, "I once hired a woman to help me reorganize my office. It took us two full days. I found myself complaining during most of the process while this woman worked diligently and ignored my gripes. I became so obsessed with the messes that I simply disregarded all the work she was putting into the project. The only thing I noticed about her was how serious and dedicated she was to completing the job. (She probably couldn't wait to be finished so she could get away from my complaining.) When we finished, I was elated and shocked. This was not the same office of days ago. It was immaculate. I suddenly realized what a difference this woman had made for my life. A neater office meant more efficiency, more time, and a greater sense of personal confidence. I turned to her, looked in her eyes, and said, 'You know, you have not only showed me how to organize, you've really changed my life. I used to walk into this office feeling so stressed I didn't even want to work. Now I feel so much better about being here. I feel motivated and confident, thanks to you.' This woman may have seemed serious before, but now she was beaming. In fact, I believe this was the first time I saw her smile."

Another benefit to complimenting is that you'll find the more compliments you give, the more come right back to you. Your life will become delightfully compliment-abundant. There is an old expression: "What comes around, goes around." I truly believe this. Why? Because when you take time to make other people's days brighter, the better you feel, the more you radiate happiness, and the greater the chances that people give warmth back to you. Try it for fun. Spend one week complimenting random people: the waiter, the unappreciated co-worker, the mailperson, whomever. Watch that positive feedback come right back.

Now, before we delve into the art of receiving the compliment, let us look at one more way to give one. In one of my flirting seminars last year, after I had explained all the specific ways to effectively pay tribute, one extremely astute woman raised her hand and said, "I think another great way to compliment is simply to tell someone you appreciate them or something they did." She was right. It means so much to a busy co-worker when you tell them, "Thanks for taking the time to explain this project to me." A new client is delighted when told, "Thanks for calling me back so promptly."

Remember my former boss Marty Domitrovich? He would always make me feel good when I arrived on time, and he noticed — "Thanks for being here right on the dot." That meant a lot to me. Simple appreciation goes so far.

Accepting the Compliment. Another way to help positive feedback come your way is to learn to accept compliments effectively. A compliment is such a wonderful gift, and yet many people seem to have so much trouble accepting them graciously. Does this dialogue sound familiar?

Susan: Jill, that suit is so flattering on you.
           Purple is your color.
Jill: This suit? I feel horrible. Nothing
           looked right on me today.

Many people automatically refute compliments. In fact, I've even seen a compliment turn into a debate.

Susan: Really, the suit looks great!
Jill: You're just saying that.
Susan: No, I'm not!

—
175

Whatever the reason, we need to stop refuting compliments and learn to accept them graciously, because we hurt several people by turning a compliment away. First, we hurt the compliment giver. It takes a lot of courage to open up to someone and say something nice. In a sense, compliment givers are handing out a gift. Take the kindness. Don't turn it away. For example, if someone says your new haircut is flattering and you don't think so, thank them anyway. By saying thanks, you make that person feel good by welcoming the compliment. Secondly, thank that person for yourself. By accepting this feedback, even if you don't initially agree, subconsciously you take in this positive comment and begin to believe it. The more compliments you accept, the more you begin to believe them. So, instead of disagreeing, from now on follow this simple rule: JUST SAY THANK YOU, AND SHUT UP! It will do wonders for you.

There is an old adage that says: "Ask and you shall receive." Good flirts have altered that quip just a bit: "Give and you shall receive."

6

TAKE ACTION!

"There are three types of people:
Those who watch things happen,
Those who make things happen,
Those who wondered what happened.

Congratulations! You've come to the last chapter and now it is time to put your flirting education to use by going out and Taking Action!
First a quick review:

FLIRTING FUNDAMENTALS

1. Eye Contact — Be sure to practice strong, direct eye contact to establish trust.

2. Be A Good Listener — Active listening is the deepest sign of appreciation.

3. Ask Open-Ended Questions — Remember, PEOPLE DON'T CARE HOW MUCH YOU KNOW UNTIL THEY KNOW HOW MUCH YOU CARE. Asking questions is a way to show that you care.

177

4. Have Confidence — People want to be with those who believe in themselves. True belief starts with you.

5. Show A Sense Of Humor — We all feel good around people who laugh at themselves and the world. Flirts laugh alot.

6. Be Honest And Sincere — Keep your word. Arrive on time. Admit your mistakes. Respect yourself so that others can respect you.

7. Like And Respect People — Being judgmental closes doors. Being open-minded opens them.

8. Stay Positive — You are what you think you are. Choose a positive attitude.

9. Be Attractive — Whatever that means to you! Beauty really does come from within.

Like yourself: Self-esteem is something to work on every day. It is you, and only you, who determines the image you want to project. Start now by being your own best coach!

Interest in others: The best way to keep the interest of others is to show interest in them. Be the best listener you can and practice empathy. Even in negotiating you keep others interested and receptive by showing them you understand their side.

Rapport through complimenting: Sincere appreciation means the world to people. And when it is directed to you, just say, "thank you," and shut up!

Take action!: So, when do you begin to put your flirting knowledge into practice? Right now! Begin by taking the first step to reach out to others. Talk to your UPS delivery person. Smile to the person you pass in the grocery store. Learn the name of the person who answered the phone at the business you just called. Listen to the passenger who sits next to you on the airplane. Laugh at yourself when you make a mistake in front of the members of the board. Greet the janitor who cleans your office. Enjoy the people and the world around you. Feeling connected with people is what flirting is all about. It's what life is all about. You will find the more you reach out, the more comes back to you.

Last week I was dining out with a colleague. When the waitress came to the table, I enthusiastically said "hi" to her as if I've known her all my life. She responded with the same warmth. "Hi! And how are *you*?" After she took our orders and left, my colleague asked me, "How do you know her?" "I don't," I explained. "But you seemed like you were great friends," he insisted. We did. Talk to someone like you know them, and you'll both feel it. Warmth is contagious. People are grateful when you reach out.

My mailman is an interesting character. For years I've watched him walk the block like a mechanical robot — dropping off, then walking, dropping off, then walking. He has a military stance and a serious expression. I admire his determination and reliability. Still, his stiff behavior suggests a lack of approachability. One day I was just leaving the house as he approached. Though his eye contact was on my mailbox, I said to him, "You have got to be the most punctual person in my life. Can I send some of my associates to you for lessons?" Still looking at my mailbox, he cracked a grin. That was that. So, what do you do when someone doesn't respond, which will occasionally happen. Remember, that it's not about you! People who don't reach back are simply not ready, so don't take it personally. Don't let your self-esteem be based on their response. Any reward involves some risk. Good for you for trying.

As for the mailman, it wasn't the most dynamic encounter I had ever had, but he had smiled. The next day it was pouring! I opened my door to get my mail, and there he was down the opposite side of the street doing his job. He saw me. I saw him. Before I flinched, a wonderful thing happened. He turned around and gave me a big wave. Well, I do believe my military mailman is flirting with me. Warmth is contagious.

The wonderful thing about flirting is that anyone can do it! No matter where you come from, what you do, or where you live, you can become an expert flirt. I can think of no better example of this than what happened to me in Jamaica one summer. I went to Negril, Jamaica, with my husband. The first day we arrived, we were standing outside our room enjoying the beautiful scenery when we noticed a man doing work in the garden nearby. He looked very hot and apparently had been working for quite some time. His clothes were very soiled and unkept and he had a dirty bandanna tied around his head. Joe and I watched him work, and he caught us watching. "Hey!" we greeted him friendly. "Yahmon!" he chirped back smiling. He rose up from his kneeled position and walked toward us. "You two just get here?" He had a delightful, strong Jamaican accent. And now close up, an endearing smile. He looked us right in the eye. And he held that warm look and a broad smile as we talked to him for a while about the island, the people, our hotel.

At times we had a bit of trouble understanding each other, but we conquered our accents and reached common ground. I found this man to be warm, confident, thoughtful, and charming. All the qualities that help build a trusting rapport. When he told us his name, I felt a sense of irony. "My name is Class." How appropriate, I thought. While he looked soiled and unkept, he had more class than most immaculately dressed professionals. True class is shown in the way you treat other people. And from the outset, he treated Joe and I with the kindest and utmost respect.

It was also interesting to see how Class interacted with his co-workers. Instead of the usual hello, Class used the word respect as his greeting. "Hey, respect Mon," he'd tell an associate. And they'd shake hands in a way I had not seen before, locking their hands around each other's thumbs and then stamping each other fist-to-fist as if in celebration. Perhaps it was a typical Jamaican custom, but I knew that for Class this was more than a greeting for him — it was a way of life.

During our stay, we spent a great deal of time with Class. He went out of his way to make us comfortable, doing extra things, which he always said was "No problem." He brought us a cassette player, since we had no music in our room and no TV. He even asked a friend who drove a cab to take us to a far away restaurant, wait for us while we ate (at no extra charge), and bring us back. Class would also check on us periodically to see if there was anything else we needed. He gave us the best service I had ever received! And none of that was related to his job, which was mainly groundwork, gardening, and cleaning up.

Class did all those extras for us because he understood the fundamentals of dealing with people. First, he loved people of all kinds and wanted to make friends. He told us stories upon stories of all the resort guests he had grown close to. People from all over — France, America, Australia. A couple from England even sent their daughter back to visit Class because they liked him so much.

The second fundamental Class understood was that the more you help others, the more it comes back to you. And it was certainly coming back to

him. Former guests who Class had befriended periodically sent him care packages or money. They
wanted to help him achieve his dream, which he
shared with us. "I want to leave this job and build a
house on the land that I own up on the hills." Each
Jamaican citizen receives a small piece of land which
is theirs to do with what they wish. Class wanted to
save enough money to build two small houses — one
for him and another to rent.

When it came time for us to leave, we were mainly
sad about leaving our new friend. Our last night of
the trip, therefore, was the perfect ending to a magi-
cal vacation. Class took us and his cab driver friend
to the hill where Class was building his dream
homes. We built a small fire and sat around it, each
of us discussing our dreams, our lives, what was
important to us. I told Class that I truly believed
one day that he would have enough money to
achieve his dream. I just knew it. After my
impromptu pep talk, I self-consciously looked down
and Class applauded. Then he gave me one of those
warm Jamaican handshakes, looked me in the eye,
and said peacefully, "Respect, Jill....Respect." We all
spoke the same language.

I conclude with this story to show that anyone can
flirt and learn to reach people. Class was a humble
gardener with a simple dream, but he understood
the importance of truly connecting with other people.
He is the epitome of a great flirt. We all can be, too.
Take action and you'll see.